THE CAT LOVER'S BOOK OF FASCINATING FACTS

The Cat Lover's Book of Fascinating Facts

A Felicitous Look at Felines

ED LUCAIRE

WINGS BOOKS
New York

This 1997 edition is published by Wings Books,
a division of Random House Value Publishing, Inc.,
201 East 50th Street, New York, NY 10022.

Wings Books and colophon are registered trademarks of
Random House Value Publishing, Inc.

RANDOM HOUSE
New York • Toronto • London • Sydney • Auckland
http://www.randomhouse.com

Printed and bound in the United States of America

Library of Congress Cataloging-in-Publication Data

Lucaire, Ed.
The cat lover's book of fascinating facts :
a felicitous look at felines / Ed Lucaire.
    p.   cm.
ISBN 0-517-15051-4
1. Cats—Miscellanea. I. Title.
SF442.L83   1997
636.8—dc20   96-34189
CIP

8 7 6 5 4 3 2

To my sister, Elvira Villegas Lucaire Hess,
a true cat lover!

ACKNOWLEDGMENTS

Special thanks to LaVonne Carlson-Finnerty, the Delta Society, Kate Hartson, Alex Hoyt, Murray Hysen, the New York Public Library, Pet Avision (*Video Catnip*), the Pet Food Institute, Ann M. Pulido, Nina Rosenstein, Rick Stromoski, Luis E. Villegas, and Alicia Waskiewicz.

Contents

I. ALL ABOUT CATS

2. FAMOUS CATS

3. A DIFFERENT BREED OF CAT
Cat Breeds and Fascinating Facts About Them

4. MISCELLANEOUS

"O lovely Pussy! O Pussy, my love,
What a beautiful Pussy you are,
You are,
You are!
What a beautiful Pussy you are!"

Sang the Owl to the Pussycat
"The Owl and the Pussycat"
EDWARD LEAR (1812–1888)

All About Cats

PHYSIOLOGY OF CATS

Cat Hearing

White cats are more prone to deafness than other cats. White cats with blue eyes are more apt to be deaf than white cats with orange eyes.

Cats have many more muscles in their ears than humans, which is why, for example, they can rotate their ears as much as 180 degrees to locate the source of a sound. (Sources vary but indicate that cats have at least ten ear muscles but possibly as many as thirty.)

Cats have one of the best senses of hearing in the animal kingdom. For starters, they can recognize the footsteps of owners from a few hundred feet. Most animals are tone deaf, but cats can distinguish between half tones. When cats hear bats fluttering their wings, it sounds like a drumroll.

When cats hear bats fluttering their
wings, it sounds like a drumroll.

Cats are especially sensitive to high-pitched sounds and can hear up to two octaves higher than the highest note that human beings can hear. A cat's skull contains two relatively large echo chambers, known as *bullae*, which are helpful in detecting high-pitched sounds that their small prey make. A cat can hear sounds as high as 50,000 cycles per second (some sources suggest higher figures) versus 40,000 c.p.s. for a dog and 20,000 c.p.s. for a human being.

When a cat purrs, the sound does not emanate from its voicebox (larynx) where its meows come from. Scientists are not sure how purrs are made, but one theory is that they are produced by a vibration of blood flowing from a vein in the chest cavity and amplified in the windpipe.

Some cats will respond to the sight and sound of television. Several companies have produced videotapes for cats that they will react to. (One of the sources is: Video Catnip, Pet Avision, Inc., P.O. Box 102, Morgantown, WV 26507-0102.)

Cats have a language but little is known about it. Studies indicate that cats have a 100 "word" vocabulary and thirteen distinct vowel sounds and seven or eight consonant sounds. It is known that mother cats make a sound that calls kittens back to the nest. Another sound communicates the size of the prey a cat is chasing. Cats have a larger "vocabulary" than dogs, according to Alphonse Leon Grimaldi, a Parisian professor.

Cat Eyesight

Cats can see six times better than human beings.

Cats cannot see any better than humans in total darkness, but they can see better under low light conditions. The cornea, pupil-hole, and lens of the cat's eye are relatively large and therefore the cat eye processes light more efficiently. Their eyes also contain more rods than cones than the human eye, favoring night vision.

The cat has a 285-degree field of vision versus 210 degrees for humans because the eyeball of a cat is shorter and rounder than that of a human, which gives it a wider field of vision. Their binocular field of vision, common to both eyes, of about 130 degrees (versus 120 degrees for humans) enables them to judge distances more accurately than people.

Cat eyes glow in the dark because of their *tapetum lucidum*, a light reflecting mechanism behind the retina.

A cat has three eyelids, the third being the nictitating membrane—thin, whitish tissue that lies at the inside corner of the eyes. When a human can see this membrane it is usually a sign that the cat is ailing.

Staring at cats provokes them and is an act of aggression. A cat can stare at another cat for extended periods of time, not necessarily resulting in a fight but a draw.

A Cat's Sense of Smell

Catnip (*Nepeta cataria*), which cats go crazy over, belongs to the garden mint family (*Labiatae*) and was once used in England as an herbal tea.

Cats under three months old have no preference for catnip and will actually avoid it. After that age, about half of cats go wild over it and the rest of them ignore it. Lions and tigers, it should also be mentioned, respond to catnip.

Catnip contains a chemical named trans-neptalactone, which strongly resembles a substance found in the urine of female cats. This is why male cats react more vigorously to catnip than female and neutered male cats do.

Cats have a sense organ that humans lack—Jacobson's organ, which is connected by duct to the roof of the mouth. It appears to be a combination smell-taste organ used in processing sexual scents of female urine by way of a process called "flehming." It involves lip curling and flaring of the nose during the evaluation of the scent-taste. (Flehming is not uncommon among other mammals.)

The cat's nose is much more sensitive—some sources indicate 30 times more sensitive—than a human's nose. A cat has almost 20 million nasal nerve endings, and a human has about 5 million.

A cat's nose is especially sensitive to the scent of nitrogen, which helps it detect and reject food and prey that is rancid. A cat with a stuffed nose may not want to eat at all.

Cats are attracted to the scent of asparagus, carnations, eucalyptus, lavender, leeks, mimosa, mint, oleander (lethal to cats, if eaten!), papyrus, pinks, silver vine, thyme, tuberoses, valerian—and, of course, catnip.

Feline Food for Thought

A cat needs about twice the percentage of protein (25 percent) in its diet than a dog needs (13 percent).

Cats are much better at stalking mice than they are at stalking birds. About 90 percent of birds escape the lunge of a cat versus only 20 percent of mice.

After a cat kills a small rodent or mammal, it swallows the prey with the grain of the hair, head first.

Cats, by nature, kill deer mice but rarely eat them. Apparently they are not palatable food.

Before a cat eats a bird, it removes its feathers. (Feathers look nice but don't taste nice, and they are virtually unswallowable.)

Americans spend almost $4 billion a year on cat food—more than they spend on baby food.

Cats are much better at stalking mice
than they are at stalking birds.

The cat tongue is predominantly raspy to enable the cat to remove as much meat as possible from the bones of its prey and to help in grooming. The abrasive part (filiform papillae) of the tongue contains no taste buds. (The taste buds lie at the tip, sides, and base of the tongue.)

Cats prefer to eat their food at 86°F, which is why they don't immediately gulp down the half-eaten can of cat food from the refrigerator.

Cats cannot digest lactose and are therefore allergic to milk, which will give them diarrhea. However, they can eat yogurt without any problems.

The milk of a mother cat contains three times the protein of cow's milk and six times the protein of human milk.

Cats love to eat liver, which is high in vitamin A, but too much of it is dangerous to the cat's life and may cause hemorrhaging and bone problems.

Aspirin, an all-purpose medicine for humans, is poisonous to cats.

Cats have an unusual preference for antifreeze (ethylene glycol) which, of course, is poisonous.

When a cat laps up water, it takes several "practice" laps before it actually swallows the liquid.

Cats require intake of more protein than most animals. Enzymes in their livers absorb much of the protein before it is used by their bodies.

Cats' tongues react to sourness and bitterness but are not sensitive to sweetness. This may be a protective device because ingesting sugar usually causes digestive problems.

Do not let your cat eat chocolate bars. They contain both theobromine, an alkaloid that is toxic to cats, and oxalic acid, which prevents absorption of calcium, necessary for the cat's bone growth and maintenance.

Toads are not the favorite prey of cats, although cats usually try to play with them and take a few bites. Toads exude a poison called bufotalin.

Don't put a litterbox near where you feed your cat. By nature, cats do not like to perform these two biological functions in the same area, and will be reluctant to eat if the litterbox is too close to their food.

Flowers and plants that are poisonous or dangerous to cats include andromeda, azalea, bittersweet, boxwood, crown of thorn, Daphne, dumb cane (*Diefenbachia*), elephant ear (*caladium*), foxglove, holly, English ivy, hydrangea, Jerusalem cherry, lantana, laurel, lily-of-the-valley, mistletoe, monkshood, oleander, philodrendron, pine needles, poinsettia, privet, rhododendron, sheep laurel, and snow-on-the-mountain.

Felinophiles Jack and Donna Wright of Kingston, Ontario, spend about $250 a day on cat food and kitty litter and $300 a day on veterinarian fees. The reason is that they own 600 cats! About their pets, the Wrights said, "We love each and every one of our six hundred cats . . . our cats are like our children."

Touch: Claws and Paws

Cats are excellent tree climbers but are extremely poor at coming down from trees because, unlike squirrels, all of their claws face forward, which makes descending almost impossible. (Most suburban firefighters, who are often called to rescue cats from trees, are aware of this fact.)

The declawing of a cat is called an "onynectomy." Declawing is a controversy among cat owners.

When a cat rubs against a person with its mouth, it is marking or leaving its scent. (Single cats rub against their owners more than cats in homes with more than one cat. Outdoor cats mark their owners more than indoor cats.)

When a cat scratches at a tree (or your furniture!) it is not only giving its claws some exercise, it is leaving its scent via the sweat on its footpads.

Originally desert animals, cats feel comfortable touching objects that are 112°F (which a human being is averse to) and can handle items as hot as 124°F without aversion.

Cat Hairs

Cats have three kinds of hair: down hair (the undercoat and long hairs), guard hair (topcoat), and awn hair (denser but shorter hair). Pointed breeds (e.g., Siamese, Birman, Balinese, and Himalayan) have darker hair on their points—the nose, ears, paws, and tail. In hotter weather their points are lighter and turn darker under cooler temperatures.

When a cat arches its back, bares its teeth, and raises its hair (piloerection), it is using a defensive technique to scare away an opponent.

A cat's whiskers (vibrissae) are usually as wide as its body and are instrumental in helping them navigate. The average cat has 24 whiskers, 12 on each side.

Cat Walk

Cats walk like giraffes and camels, which is to say that they move the front and hind legs on one side and then move forward the front and hind legs on the other side. (Most animals move one front leg forward at the same time they move the opposite rear leg forward.)

The domestic cat, a natural sprinter, can run as fast as thirty miles an hour versus twenty-two m.p.h. for an extremely fast hundred-yard dash human runner.

The heaviest cat on record was Himmy, a
neutered male tabby from Australia.

Cat Size

Cat breeds vary less in shape and size than dog breeds do because cats have a less varied genetic makeup. The cat has only been selectively bred for less than a hundred years, whereas dogs have been selectively bred for specific characteristics (e.g., hunting ability) for centuries. (Dogs were domesticated 50,000 years ago versus 4,000-plus years ago for cats.)

The average female domestic cat weighs six to ten pounds and the average male domestic cat weighs ten to fifteen pounds. The weights of dogs vary significantly more. A Saint Bernard, for example, weighs about 300 times what a little Yorkshire terrier weighs.

The heaviest cat on record was Himmy, a neutered male tabby from Australia. It weighed forty-six pounds, fifteen and one quarter ounces when it died in 1986 at age ten years and four months.

At age twenty-three months, a male Siamese cat named Ebony, owned by Angelina Johnston of Boise, Idaho, weighed only one pound and twelve ounces, as of February 1984.

The Maine Coon and Ragdoll tend to be the heaviest domestic breeds of cat, averaging between fifteen and twenty pounds.

The Singapura is the smallest breed of domestic cat. The average Singapura male weighs six pounds and the average female weighs three pounds.

General Cat Health and Physiology

Bad breath in a cat may be due to dental problems but it also may be due to kidney problems, when the body is not excreting properly.

The average cat has a heart rate of 110 to 130 beats per minute (compared to seventy-five beats per minute for a human being). A cat's heart can beat as rapidly as 240 beats per minute when excited.

About 10 percent of the cats in New England, New Brunswick, Canada, and Nova Scotia have an extra toe.

The average lifespan of a cat is fifteen years, but the oldest cat on record was Puss, a tabby from Devon, England. It reached its thirty-sixth birthday on November 28, 1939, but died the next day. Coincidentally, another Devon tabby lived to the age of thirty-four, when it was put to sleep on November 28, 1939.

Cats have "belly buttons," although they do not resemble human navels. They appear as an elongated scar, covered by hair.

As cat lovers have always known, the cat is a very intelligent animal. Using one physiological standard (brain weight to spinal cord length), the cat brain has a ratio of four to one (versus fifty to one for humans and eighteen to one for monkeys.) Cats have a memory ability superior to monkeys and orangutans.

Dogs rely heavily on their senses of smell and touch for daily existence, but cats rely mostly on sights and sounds.

The nucleus of a cat cell has thirty-eight chromosomes, or nineteen pairs, versus forty-six (twenty-three pairs) for the nucleus of a human cell.

Cat naps add up to the "big sleep." Cats sleep about sixteen hours a day, off and on, twice a human's requirement, and more than any other mammal.

Cats lack water-producing (eccrine) sweat glands except on their footpads. Their apocrine sweat glands produce a milky substance that is used in marking territory and leaving scents.

Cats not only can be left-handed ("left-pawed"), but they are more apt to be left-handed than humans. In a study by Dr. J. Cole at Oxford University, England, 38 percent of the cats studied were exclusively left-handed and an additional 20 percent had left-handed tendencies, leaving 42 percent of them right-handed. (About 10 percent of humans are left-handed.)

Cats lack a collarbone, or clavicle. This enables them to walk through narrow spaces and to take long strides.

Cats can lose a lot of body weight (40 percent) and still survive, but they can't lose more than 14 percent of water and live.

The intestines of a cat are short—only four times the length of its body, relatively shorter than the intestines of humans and dogs.

Domestic cats cover up their excrement but wild cats do not—to the contrary, cats in the wild leave their feces and urine in conspicuous places.

Feline ESP (Extra Sensory Perception)

Cats have an extraordinary ability to sense imminent earthquakes, usually ten to fifteen minutes before they actually occur. They exhibit nervous behavior such as pawing or scratching at doors and windows, and above-average concern with the safety of kittens. One theory is that cats' footpads are extremely sensitive to vibrations and sound waves. Other theories suggest that cats are sensitive to shifts in static electricity or the earth's magnetic field, both of which occur during earthquakes.

THE SEX LIFE OF CATS

Male cats have small barbs, or papillae, on their penises to stimulate ovulation in the female and to help hold the female in place.

Ovulation in humans and dogs occurs spontaneously but with cats it is male penetration that triggers ovulation.

More than one tomcat can impregnate a female during the same period of ovulation. The phenomenon is called superfecundation or multiple impregnation.

The average length of a cat's penis is three quarters of an inch—longer than a mosquito's penis (1/100th of an inch) but shorter than a gorilla's (two inches!).

Sexual intercourse between domestic cats usually takes only a few seconds and almost never longer than fifteen seconds. A pair may mate six to twelve times an hour.

A pair of cats theoretically could produce a population of 65,536 cats in five years, according to zoologist and author Desmond Morris in his book *Catwatching*. To arrive at this number, he assumed three litters a year of fourteen kittens, with no deaths, sterility, or neuterings.

In cat hierarchy, once a female is neutered it loses its social rank, as does a castrated tomcat.

A neutered tomcat lives an average of three years longer than an unneutered one.

It is believed that a tomcat's amount of territory is more important than sexual prowess or physical strength in determining which male cats females choose as sexual partners.

Older un-neutered female cats that never have had a litter may suffer from apparent nymphomania—being in perpetual heat. They are suffering from the disease endometrial hyperplasia-pyometra complex.

Cats are subject to Feline Immunodeficiency Virus (FIV), a disease similar to AIDS (acquired immune deficiency syndrome). Fortunately, FIV cannot be transmitted from cats to humans.

CATS AS SURVIVORS

When the Dutch ship *Tjoba* sank in December 1964, the crew was saved but the ship's cat, Jacob, was an apparent fatality. A week later the ship was raised with a giant crane and winch, and the crew went aboard to claim their belongings. The captain opened his cabin door, only to find a bedraggled and shivering Jacob, who apparently survived in a pocket of trapped air.

A cat locked in a Cadillac being shipped by freight from the United States to Australia survived fifty-two days without eating food—by licking engine grease and eating the car instruction manual.

A cat named Chips from Liverpool was accidentally put in a crate and shipped to Mombassa, Africa. It survived the four-week voyage apparently because it licked the condensation and grease off the machinery packed in the crate.

A cat named Kelly was locked in a cold Brownwood, Texas, storeroom for forty-six days in early 1990 and managed to survive.

A stray cat named Scarlett made New York news in late March 1996 when it jeopardized its own life five times by repeatedly walking into a burning abandoned garage to save its five kittens. Almost singed to death, the cat was given the name Scarlett by the press because it was so badly burned that its oozing skin was exposed. Although Scarlett's eyes looked severely damaged, Dr. Larry Cohen, a Long Island veterinarian, felt that the cat's corneas were in sufficient shape to recover sight.

Yes, cats can fall from great heights and still survive.

Yes, cats can fall from great heights and still survive. A cat named Gros Minou fell two stories from a Quebec suburb apartment house in May 1973. The cat fell over 200 feet and broke its pelvis, but fully recovered in a couple of months.

High-rise feline falls are not uncommon. In 1994, two cats owned by Harvey Pedersen of Rockaway Beach, New York, fell off his eleventh floor balcony and survived. Kitty fell and disappeared, but emerged from a drain two months later. Shortly thereafter, Stinky fell from the same balcony and was quickly retrieved off some hedges at ground level—with no apparent injuries.

Veterinarian Dr. Michael Garvey attributes this unusual survival phenomenon to "high-rise syndrome," in which cats falling from greater heights are more apt to survive because they have time to relax and land prepared, almost like a parachutist.

TERRITORIALITY AND THE CAT

When spraying its urine to mark territory, a male cat will make the same number of squirts whether it has a full bladder or empty bladder.

Dogs mark territory with their urine for other dogs to detect. Cats also do the same thing, but cat markings differ in that they also tell other cats how recently they left their marks.

The territory of a female cat is about one-tenth the size of a male's territory.

The territory of an indoor cat may be as small as a section of a room or a mere armchair or couch. A domestic outdoor cat may have a territory as large as 175 acres or only one-fifth of an acre in an urban setting.

FELINE FIRSTS

The first cat show was held at the famous Crystal Palace on July 13, 1871. Organized by Victorian artist and writer Harrison Weir, the show featured about 160 cats.

The first American photographer of cats was Charles Bullar, whose feline photographs began appearing in the late 1880s.

The first domesticated cat specifically named in literature is Pangur Bán (Gaelic for "white cat"), about whom an eighth-century Irish monk and scholar wrote:

> I and Pangur Bán my cat,
> 'Tis a like task we are at;
> Hunting mice is his delight
> Hunting words I sit all night . . .

The first cat to win a Patsy award, the animal equivalent of an Academy Award, was Orangey, who played the title role in the 1951 movie *Rhubarb*. The movie also starred Ray Milland and was based on the story by H. Allen Smith about a cat that inherits a baseball team. (See "Oscar" Winning Cats)

CATS AS HEALERS AND THERAPISTS

Medical researchers have proved that cats (and other pets) have salutary effects on the elderly, the handicapped, and institutionalized people.

In 1977 Drs. Aaron Katcher and Erica Friedmann of the University of Pennsylvania studied the recoveries of heart-attack victims and found that those with pets were more apt to recover and stabilize their health (e.g., lower heart rate, lower blood pressure) than those without pets. In fact, the heart patients without pets showed a proclivity for having additional attacks, some resulting in death. Medical tests prove that simply petting a cat tends to lower one's blood pressure.

Drs. Samuel and Elizabeth Corson of the Department of Psychiatry at Ohio State University, proponents of pet therapy, maintain that pets "act as a catalyst for feelings which are eventually transferred to other people." Psychologist David Greene, author of the insightful book *Your Incredible Cat*, notes that pets "provide an outlet for emotions which might otherwise remain blocked," and serve "as a bridge between the outright rejection and gradual acceptance of personal relationships." Dr. Gerald Lowbeer, a British psychiatrist, believes that patients feel dependent and passive and that care of a cat makes them feel more active and care-giving.

In 1976 a ten-year-old girl named Marie from outside Mazatlan, Mexico, was struck by a car and went into a coma for months. A stray black cat, soon to be named Mogul, entered her room through an open window one day, jumped on her bed, snuggled by her left arm, and began licking the child's thumb. Marie's mother noted a slight movement in her fingers, the first movement since the accident. Eight days later Marie came out of the coma and began uttering words. She eventually recovered but Mogul mysteriously disappeared, not staying to share the joys of Marie's renewed life.

LONG DISTANCE CATS

Cats have an amazing ability to find their way home. Some of the stories sound difficult to believe, but researchers at Duke University, Drs. Joseph Rhine and Sara Feather, have verified dozens of similar stories that cat owners have passed on through the years. It is believed that cats have a celestial navigation system similar to that of birds, primarily using the angle of sunlight or, on overcast days, the angle of polarized light. Here are a few examples of a cat's incredible homing instinct:

While on vacation in Wales, London resident Margaret Adams was devastated on learning that her cat Sampson had disappeared. Two years later, she saw a cat resembling Sampson on her property and called his name. He sallied forth and Ms. Adams verified his unusual markings. It was, in fact, Sampson, who had taken a leisurely two years to amble over 250 miles.

A Persian cat named How, owned by fifteen-year-old Kristen Hicks of Adelaide, Australia, was left with her grandparents in the Outback 1,000 miles away when the family went overseas. When Kristen and her parents returned to Australia months later, they learned that her cat had mysteriously disappeared. Almost a year later a weather-beaten Persian cat showed up at the Hicks' doorstep in Adelaide. Howie had walked a few miles a day to return to his real home.

A kitten named Pitchou left his home in Merlebach and managed to find his owner Fernand Schmitt about seventy-five miles away by following the tracks on which Schmitt took a train back to his barracks in Strasbourg in northeast France.

Lafayette, Louisiana, cat Beau Chat, a white half-Persian, vanished when his owners took a trip to Texarkana, Texas, in late 1953 and left him home. The cat reappeared four months later at the school where the family's eight-year-old son, Butchie, was a student and his mother was a teacher.

Cat-owner Brenda James returned to her home one night after attending a play, and found that her house had been burglarized. Missing were her TV, money, silver items, and her beloved red tabby cat, Cindy. Much distraught, she tried to locate the cat without success and gave up her search. Over two years later in her new house, three miles from her previous residence, her neighbor found a forlorn cat on James's front step. It was long-lost Cindy.

In 1949 a cat named Rusty left Boston, Massachusetts, and found its owner in Chicago, almost 1,000 miles away, a trip made in only eighty-three days.

Lafayette, Louisiana, cat Beau Chat, vanished in late 1953 when his owners took a trip and left him home. The cat reappeared four months later at the school attended by the family's son.

A half-Persian cat named Sugar, who easily became carsick, was left with a neighbor in Anderson, California, when its owner Mary moved to Oklahoma, about 1,500 miles away. Sugar's new owner called two weeks later to tell Mary that the cat had disappeared. Over a year later Sugar mysteriously appeared while Mary was doing garden work outside her new home. The two had a joyful reunion.

A homesick tabby named McCavity walked from Cumbermauld, the location of his new home, to his hometown near Truro, Cornwall, a distance of about 500 miles, in only three weeks.

According to Dr. Michael Fox, a cat named Tom traveled about 2,500 miles from St. Petersburg, Florida, to San Gabriel, California, to find its owner, who had moved.

CAT ACHIEVEMENTS

A British tabby named Mickey (a.k.a. Mickie or Micky) killed a record 22,000 mice while a "mouser" for Shepherd & Sons, Ltd., for whom the cat worked for twenty-three years. He died in 1968, comfortable in the knowledge that he made the pages of the *Guinness Book of World Records* as the "Mousing Champion." Records, however, are made to be broken, and a new record was set by Towser, a female tortoiseshell, which killed 28,899 mice at the Glenturret Distillery outside Scotland. Towser pounced on an average of three mice per day until her death on March 20, 1987.

The champion "ratter" on record was Minnie, a female tabby who killed 12,480 rats at White City Stadium in England from 1927 to 1933.

A cat helped build the Grand Coulee Dam in Columbia, Washington. In order to install electric cables, engineers tied string to the cat's tail and made it walk through a long winding drainpipe. The string was then tied to a rope, which was also pulled through the pipe. Finally the rope was tied to a cable, which was pulled through the system, thereby accomplishing the mission of wiring the system.

In Buenos Aires in the late 1940s, a black female cat named Mincha climbed a forty-foot tree and stayed up there for six years. Local residents sent food up to the cat with long poles.

Some scientists, such as animal researcher André Marcal of France and Dr. Leon Smith, inventor of the Behavioral Engineering Technique (BET), believe that cats can replace humans for many tasks, including assembly line work, operation of electronic equipment, and household chores.

KITTENS AND MOTHERS

A mother cat is known as a queen or a dam.

The record number of offspring by one female cat is held by a seventeen-year-old cat named Dusty, which gave birth to 420 kittens in her lifetime.

A newborn kitten attaches itself to a specific nipple of the mother and continues to return to it based on its sense of smell. The other kittens in the brood establish similar attachments to the mother's other nipples.

Sometimes adult cats knead on the chest of their owners or on a blanket or pillow—it is a "milk-treading" behavior that kittens exhibit while nursing, apparently to help stimulate milk flow.

Newborn kittens will not urinate or defecate unless the mother licks the kittens' abdomens and perineal area. The mother will then consume the kittens' excretions. When they are about three weeks old, they are able to perform these functions without maternal stimulation, and take care of their own cleanliness.

A four-month-old kitten climbed to the top of the 14,691-foot-high Matterhorn on the Swiss-Italian border in 1950. The cat was owned by Josephine Aufdenblatten of Geneva, Switzerland.

Famous Cats

FAMOUS CAT LOVERS

The Greek historian Herodotus used the word *ailourus* ("the waving ones") for cats. The modern term for cat lover is *ailourophile*. Here is a long list of famous cat lovers, past and present:

Aesop (*fabulist*)
St. Agatha (*"Santo Gato" or Saint Cat*)
Loni Anderson (*television actress*)
Cleveland Amory (*author and animal rights activist*)
Charles Baudelaire (*French poet*)
Orson Bean (*humorist, actor*)
Jeremy Bentham (*British philosopher*)
Ambrose Bierce (*writer*)
Otto von Bismarck (*German statesman*)
Amanda Black (*actress*)
Ray Bradbury (*science fiction author*)
Anne Brontë (*British writer*)

Charlotte Brontë (British writer)

Emily Brontë (British writer)

Samuel Butler (British writer)

Lord Byron (British poet)

Karle Capek (Czechoslovakian playwright)

Roger Caras (author, broadcaster)

Claudia Cardinale (Italian film actress)

Thomas Carlyle (Scottish writer, historian)

Lewis Carroll (British writer)

Raymond Chandler (detective novelist)

Vicomte de Chateaubriand (French writer, politician)

Lord Chesterfield (British statesman)

Sir Winston Churchill (British prime minister)

Georges Clemenceau (French prime minister)

Jean Cocteau (French writer)

Colette (French writer)

Confucius (Chinese religious leader)

Robin Cook (writer)

Calvin Coolidge (U.S. president)

Gustave Courbet (French artist)

William Cowper (British writer, hymnologist)

Countee Cullen (poet)

Sandy Dennis (actress)

Bo Derek (actress)

Benjamin Disraeli (British politician)

Alexander Dumas (French writer)

Albert Einstein (physicist)

T. S. Eliot (writer)

Erté (designer)

Pope Leo XII and his cats

Nanette Fabray (*actress*)

Anatole France (*French writer*)

Anne Frank (*Dutch diarist*)

Benjamin Franklin (*politician and inventor*)

Eva Gabor (*actress*)

Paul Gallico (*writer*)

Théophile Gautier (*French writer*)

William Gladstone (*British statesman*)

John Gay (*English poet*)

Edward Gorey (*artist*)

Francisco Goya (*Spanish artist*)

Thomas Gray (*English poet*)

Pope Gregory the Great (*religious leader*)

Pope Gregory III (*religious leader*)

Peggy Guggenheim (*heiress, arts patron*)

Thomas Hardy (*British writer*)

Ernest Hemingway (*writer*)

Victor Hugo (*French writer*)

King James I of England (*son of Mary, Queen of Scots*)

Henry James (*British writer*)

Ingres, Jean-Auguste-Dominique (*French painter*)

Thomas Jefferson (*U.S. president*)

Samuel Johnson (*lexicographer*)

B. Kliban (*artist*)

Edward Lear (*British writer*)

General Robert E. Lee (*U.S. military leader*)

Vladimir Lenin (*Russian leader*)

Pope Leo XII (*religious leader*)

Abraham Lincoln (*U.S. president*)

Sophia Loren (Italian actress)

King Louis XV of France

Martin Luther (religious leader)

Sir Compton Mackenzie (British writer)

Anna Magnani (Italian actress)

Stephane Mallarmé (French poet)

Edouard Manet (French painter)

Marie Antoinette (French monarch)

Saint Martha (1st century A.D. religious leader)

James Mason (British actor)

Guy de Maupassant (French writer)

Prosper Mérimée (French writer)

Mohammed (Arab religious leader)

Michel Eyquem Montaigne (French writer)

H. H. Munro ("Saki") (writer)

Sir Philip Neri (Italian religious leader)

Sir Isaac Newton (physicist)

Florence Nightingale (British nurse)

Peter O'Toole (Irish actor)

Louis Pasteur (medical scientist)

George S. Patton (U.S. general)

St. Patrick (patron saint of Ireland)

Jane Pauley (television journalist)

Petrarch (Italian poet)

Pablo Picasso (Spanish artist)

Pope Pius VII (religious leader)

Edgar Allan Poe (writer)

Beatrix Potter (British author, illustrator)

Madame Récamier (French social leader)

Rembrandt (Dutch artist)

Maurice Ravel (French composer)

Auguste Renoir (French artist)

Cardinal Richelieu (religious leader)

Tanya Roberts (actress)

Franklin D. Roosevelt (U.S. president)

Theodore Roosevelt (U. S. president)

Jean-Jacques Rousseau (French philosopher)

May Sarton (Belgian-American Poet)

Albert Schweitzer (Alsatian physician, missionary)

George Bernard Shaw (British playwright)

Christopher Smart (English poet)

Robert Southey (English poet laureate)

Madame de Staël (French writer)

Theodore Steinlein (artist)

Algernon Charles Swinburne (writer)

Booth Tarkington (writer)

Elizabeth Taylor (actress)

James Taylor (singer)

Ellen Terry (British actress)

William Makepeace Thackeray (writer)

J. R. R. Tolkien (writer)

Henry David Thoreau (philosopher)

James Thurber (humorist)

Gary Trudeau (cartoonist)

Mark Twain (writer)

Mark Van Doren (writer)

Jules Verne (author)

Queen Victoria (British monarch)

Horace Walpole (British writer)

H. G. Wells (British writer)

Jessamyn West (writer)

Cardinal Wolsey (British religious leader, politician)

P .G. Wodehouse (British writer)

William Butler Yeats (Irish writer, poet)

Emile Zola (French writer)

FAMOUS CAT HATERS

Fortunately for cats and their owners, hatred or fear of cats (ailurophobia) is much less common than love of cats (ailurophilia). It is worth noting that most cat haters are "control freaks" or people with strong dictatorial and tyrannical streaks. The theory is that these people, by their nature, are averse to any human or animal that does not immediately respond to their demands. The following notables are among those known to hate or fear cats.

French sonneteer Pierre de Ronsard (1524–1585), the court poet of Charles IX, wrote the following bitter words about cats:

> There is no man now living anywhere,
> Who hates cats with a deeper hate than I;
> I hate their eyes, their heads, the way they stare,
> And when I see one come, I turn and fly.

U.S. President Dwight D. Eisenhower (1890–1969) was not very fond of cats or crows, according to his grandson and biographer David Eisenhower. At his Gettysburg, Pennsylvania, home, Ike kept a shotgun handy to shoot crows and ordered that any cats found roaming on the property should be shot.

Scottish author James Boswell (1740–1795), biographer of cat lover and lexicographer Samuel Johnson, hated cats.

When not writing music, German composer Johannes Brahms (1833–1897) liked to shoot neighborhood cats with a bow and arrow.

Georges de Buffon (1707–1788), French naturalist and author of *Histoire Naturelle*, wrote that the cat is a "deceitful character" with a "perverse nature that grows worse with age and which education only disguises."

Cats were routinely burned to death during the reign of Mary (Blood Mary) Tudor from 1553 to 1558 as a sign of Protestant heresy.

Queen Elizabeth I (who reigned from 1558 to 1603) disliked both cats and Roman Catholics. When she was coronated she had an effigy of the Pope constructed and then had it filled with live cats. When the effigy was set afire, the deathly screaming of the cats was horrific and Elizabeth strongly conveyed her dislikes.

Henry III, King of France, fainted whenever a cat came too close to him.

French emperor Napoleon Bonaparte (1769–1821) broke into a sweat whenever a cat or kitten was nearby.

When not writing music, German composer
Johannes Brahms liked to shoot
neighborhood cats with a bow and arrow.

Pope Innocent VIII declared war on heresy and announced in 1484 that witches and their feline companions would be burned at the stake.

In his famous dictionary, American lexicographer Noah Webster (1758–1843) wrote that the cat is a "deceitful animal and when enraged extremely spiteful."

Other cat haters include Alexander the Great (356–323 B.C.), French-born British writer (and Napoleon biographer) Hilaire Belloc (1870–1953), German composer Giacomo Meyerbeer (1791–1864), Mongol conqueror Genghis Khan (1162–1227), Italian dictator Benito Mussolini (1883–1945), and Roman emperor Julius Caesar (100–44 B.C.) According to author Roger Caras, Adolf Hitler (1899–1945) was also a cat hater.

FAMOUS FELINE FACTS
AND ANECDOTES

Movie director and producer Steven Spielberg got the idea for the television series *E.R.* when he rushed a Siamese cat that had fallen out of a window to a hospital. Michael Crichton, a Harvard Medical School graduate and author of many books, including *Jurassic Park*, was a logical partner for Spielberg to develop the show with.

When missionary doctor Albert Schweitzer's cat Sizi nestled by his left arm, Schweitzer, who was left-handed, wrote with his right hand.

King Charles I of England owned a black cat, which he considered his good luck charm. After the cat died, Charles announced, "My luck is gone!" and he was right. The following day he was arrested and shortly thereafter executed (beheaded!) by Oliver Cromwell.

Muslim founder and prophet Mohammed often carried a cat, his favorite being Muezza ("prayer" in Arabic). The cat is described in the Koran as a pure animal and was blessed (the dog was considered an impure one). The classic story is that Muezza was once asleep at the prophet's arm when Mohammed had to go pray, so he cut off the sleeve of his robe rather than disturb the revered cat.

John Kenneth Galbraith, the Canadian-born economist and U.S. ambassador to India, created a stir in India when his family addressed their cat by the name Mohammed, which offended Islamic Indians. (He actually had named the cat Ahmedabad, after the capital city of the Indian state of Gujarat.) When the dust had finally settled, he and his family called the cat Gujarat.

Some sources indicate that English poet Percy Bysshe Shelley once tied a cat to a kite and flew it during a thunderstorm, for reasons not stated. Given that Shelley was a writer (they tend to be cat lovers) and not a crazed Transylvanian scientist, it is highly doubtful that this story is true.

Pioneer British nurse Florence Nightingale owned dozens of cats, and usually gave them the names of famous people such as Disraeli, Gladstone, and Bismarck.

Cardinal Richelieu, the French politician, owned fourteen cats and loved them enough to provide for them in his will.

French novelist George Sand (née Aurore Dudevant) had no qualms about drinking from the same cup that her cat drank from.

British prime minister Winston Churchill owned several cats, including ones named Blackie, Margate, Tango, Jock, and Nelson, the latter named after the famous British admiral. About Nelson, who allegedly hid under the ministerial bed during the London blitz, Churchill commented, "Despite my most earnest and eloquent entreaties, I failed most utterly in persuading my friend before taking such craven action to give even passing consideration to the name he bore."

Before his transatlantic flight, Charles Lindbergh was photographed in the cockpit of his plane with a kitten named Patsy. A stamp was issued also showing the cat. Contrary to popular belief, however, the kitten did not accompany him on his flight to Paris.

British author Aldous Huxley advised aspiring young writers to buy a lot of paper, pen, and ink—and a pair of cats!

While performing at London's St. James Theatre, Polish pianist Ignace Paderewski was visited by the cat that lived in the theater. It jumped on Paderewski's lap and the pianist continued playing his opening number.

St. Patrick, the patron saint of Ireland and a cat lover, began the tradition of Irish monks' breeding cats.

Cardinal Richelieu, the French politician, owned fourteen cats and loved them enough to provide for them in his will.

French writer Victor Hugo had a special throne-like chair built for his cat.

English lexicographer and cat lover Samuel Johnson, according to his biographer James Boswell (a cat hater), fed oysters to his cat Hodge.

Author Charles Dickens owned a cat named William, but when he discovered that it was a female cat he renamed it Williamina. Dickens was not a cat lover, by the way, but after evicting Williamina and her kittens several times (they kept returning) he finally accepted them.

French writer Alexander Dumas was once described as the "defense lawyer of cats around the world," and owned the equivalent of a small zoo.

French world chess champion (1927–1935) Alexander Alekhine liked to play chess with his cat on his lap, which annoyed opponents. At a major tournament in 1935 the judges ruled that his cat could not be present during the match.

In Key West, Florida, writer Ernest Hemingway kept as many as thirty cats at one time. He brought many of them back from his finca (farm) in Cuba to mate with his American-born cats. His Key West house, now a museum, still teems with felines.

General Robert E. Lee, during the Mexican war, asked his family to send him a cat to keep him company.

English philosopher and mathematician Isaac Newton is credited with inventing the cat "door" or holes in doors, called gatera in Spain and chatiere in France.

French composer Maurice Ravel ("Bolero") owned over thirty cats.

When Italian poet Petrarch's (1304–1374) cat died, it was mummified and entombed with the inscription "Second only to Laura," the latter being a woman whom Petrarch loved. The cat was buried above his doorway to ward off evil spirits. Its remains now lie at a museum in Padua, Italy.

Nancy Seaver, wife of former baseball pitcher Tom Seaver, named her cat Ferguson after another baseball pitcher— Ferguson Jenkins.

French writer Colette (*Gigi* and *The Cat*), an inveterate cat lover, played the role of a cat in *La Chatte Amoureuse* on the stage in 1912.

Singer Roberta Flack named her cat after another famous singer—Caruso.

Spanish playwright Lope de Vega (*Fuenteovejuna*) wrote a piece entitled *Gattomachia* (Battle Among Cats) in which he ridicules people and praises cats.

Edgar Allan Poe often wrote while his cat Catalina was perched on his left shoulder. In fact, the nineteenth-century artist Charles Smeldon drew a portrait of Poe with quill in hand and Catalina nestled on his shoulder.

U.S. PRESIDENTS AND THEIR CATS

U.S. presidents are more apt (two to one) to own dogs, but some of them owned cats.

Although GEORGE WASHINGTON owned mostly dogs, Martha Washington had a special miniature door built into her bedroom door at Mount Vernon to let her cats come and go as they pleased.

ABRAHAM LINCOLN's son Tad kept a kitten named Tabby at the White House.

RUTHERFORD B. HAYES and his wife "Lemonade" Lucy owned four kittens. A diplomat from Siam (David B. Sickels) gave Lucy a Siamese kitten named Miss Pussy, which they immediately renamed Siam.

WILLIAM McKINLEY and his wife Ida owned an Angora cat. When the cat gave birth to four kittens, Ida named the weaker of the cats Valeriano Weyler, after the governor of Cuba, and Enrique DeLome, after the Spanish ambassador. (She ordered her maid to drown the two cats when the war with Spain was not going well.)

THEODORE ROOSEVELT owned a cat named Tom Quartz, a feisty and fluffy feline named for a cat in Mark Twain's *Roughing It*, and a six-toed cat named Slippers. In fact, it was President Roosevelt who helped popularize cat ownership in America.

WOODROW WILSON owned a white cat named Puffins. (Wilson, by the way, was an avid reader of George Harriman's "Krazy Kat" comic strip, as were publisher William Randolph Hearst and writer e.e. cummings.)

CALVIN COOLIDGE owned many dogs and at least three cats: Blackie, Bounder, and the striped Tiger.

JOHN F. KENNEDY's daughter Caroline owned a kitten named Tom Kitten, named after author Beatrix Potter's feline character. However, JFK was allergic to it and it was given to Jacqueline's secretary Mary Gallagher, who renamed the cat Tom Terrific.

GERALD R. FORD went to the White House with a Siamese cat named Chan, who was daughter Susan's pet.

In his childhood, JIMMY CARTER owned a dog named Bozo. When the Carters moved to 1600 Pennsylvania Avenue, one of Amy's teachers gave her a puppy, which she named Grits. Grits and the White House didn't get along and it was returned to its original purchaser. Among other things, Grits could not get along with Amy Carter's Siamese cat Misty Malarkey Ying Yang.

BILL CLINTON's daughter Chelsea's cat, Socks, was given to her by her piano teacher. Chelsea chose the cat over its sibling Midnight because she liked the white toes of the cat, hence the name Socks.

BLACK CATS AND
THEIR OWNERS

Writer Edgar Allan Poe wasn't the first person to malign black cats but he certainly didn't make them more popular, except as cinematic stereotypes for additional horror stories and movies.

For example, Pope Gregory IX, a notorious cat hater, believed that followers of the devil kissed the genital area of black cats before they embarked on evil orgies.

Superstition often accompanies fame—actors and actresses are among the most superstitious beings on Earth. Perhaps they know that fame is often fleeting.

Nevertheless, here are some intrepid notables of the past and present who have not been afraid of owning a black cat:

> **Roger Caras** (author/broadcaster)
> **Thomas Carlyle** (Scottish historian and essayist)
> **Winston S. Churchill** (British statesman)
> **John Spencer Churchill** (Churchill's father)
> **Calvin Coolidge** (U.S. President)
> **Lou Costello** (comedic actor)
> **Elvira** (television and movie vamp)
> **Théophile Gautier** (French writer)
> **Deirdre Hall** (actress)
> **Harry Hamlin** (actor)
> **P. D. James** (author)
> **Gertrude Lawrence** (actress)

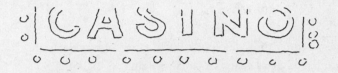

**Black cats are considered good luck
in Great Britain.**

Alicia Markova (*ballerina*)
Yoko Ono (*musician and artist*)
Robert Southey (*writer*)
Elizabeth Taylor (*actress*)
Joan Van Ark (*actress*)
Betty White (*actress*)

P.S. According to psychologist David Greene, black cats are regarded as a *good* omen in Great Britain.

FELINE FLICKS: CATS IN THE CINEMA

Az Prijde Kocour (1963)
A Czech movie about a cat that, according to the review in *The New York Times*, "wears magic glasses through which it sees deceptive and cautious people in their true colors."

The Black Cat (1934)
A horror film that bears no resemblance to Edgar Allan Poe's classic short story, starring Boris Karloff, Bela Lugosi, David Manners, Jacqueline Wells, Lucille Lund, Henry Armetta, and Harry Cording.

The Black Cat (1941)
A comedic mystery starring Basil Rathbone, Hugh Herbert, Broderick Crawford, Bela Lugosi, Gale Sondergaard, Anne Gwynne, and Gladys Cooper. Future star Alan Ladd appears briefly.

The Black Cat (1966)
Starring Robert Frost and Robyn Baker, this version was fairly faithful to the Edgar Allan Poe short story.

The Bluebird (1940)
A fantasy based on Maurice Maeterlinck's play about children seeking "the bluebird of happiness," starring Shirley Temple, Spring Byington, Nigel Bruce, Gale Sondergaard, Eddie Collins, and Sybil Jason.

The Bluebird (1976)
A remake of the 1940 version of the Maeterlinck play and joint U. S.–Russian production, starring Todd Lookinland, Patsy Kensit, Elizabeth Taylor, Jane Fonda, Ava Gardner, Cicely Tyson, George Cole, Will Geer, Robert Morley, and Harry Andrews.

Breakfast at Tiffany's (1961)
Based on Truman Capote's novella and starring Audrey Hepburn, George Peppard, Mickey Rooney, Patricia Neal, Buddy Ebsen, Martin Balsam, John McGiver, and a cat named Cat (played by Rhubarb, a.k.a. Orangey).

The Cat (1966)
Starring Roger Perry, Peggy Ann Garner, Barry Coe, and Dwayne Redlin. About a lost boy threatened by a cattle rustler but rescued by a friendly wildcat.

The Cat and the Canary (1927)
Based on the 1922 stage play by John Willard, a comedic horror story that starred Laura LaPlante, Tully Marshall, Flora Finch, Creighton Hale, Gertrude Astor, and Lucien Littlefield.

The Cat and the Canary (1939)
A comedic remake of the 1927 movie, starring Bob Hope (his first major role), Paulette Goddard, Gale Sondergaard, John Beal, Douglass Montgomery, Nydia Westman, and George Zucco.

The Cat and the Canary (1978)
A British comedy-mystery production that starred Honor Blackman, Michael Callan, Edward Fox, Wendy Hiller, Olivia Hussey, Carol Lynley, Peter McEnery, and Wilfred Hyde-White.

The Cat and the Fiddle (1934)
Based on the Jerome Kern and Oscar Hammerstein operetta, this comedy starred Jeanette MacDonald, Ramon Novarro, Frank Morgan, Charles Butterworth, and Jean Hersholt.

Cat Ballou (1965)
A popular mid-1960s comedy starring Jane Fonda, Lee Marvin (who won the Oscar for best actor), Nat King Cole, Stubby Kaye, Michael Callan, and Dwayne Hickman.

The Cat Creeps (1930)
The first sound version of *The Cat and the Canary*, it starred Helen Twelvetrees, Raymond Hackett, Neil Hamilton, and Jean Hersholt.

The Cat Creeps (1946)
Not related to the 1930 movie, this film starred Noah Beery Jr., Lois Collier, Paul Kelly, Douglass Dumbrille, and Fred Bradt.

The Cat From Outer Space (1978)
About an alien Abyssinian cat that lands on earth to fix its space ship, starring Scott Berry, Sandy Duncan, Harry Morgan, Roddy McDowall, and McLean Stevenson.

Cat Girl (1957)
A horror film starring Barbara Shelley about a woman who thinks she is cursed and will become a leopard.

Cat People (1942)
A horror movie starring Simone Simon, Kent Smith, Tom Conway, Jack Holt, and Jane Randolph. Smith falls in love with Simon, who has the curse of a panther inside her.

Cat People (1982)
A loose remake of the 1942 movie starring Nastassia Kinski, Malcolm McDowell, John Heard, Annette O'Toole, Ruby Dee, Ed Begley Jr., Scott Paulin, and John Larroquette.

Eye of the Cat (1969)
A suspense thriller starring Michael Sarrazin, Gayle Hunnicut, Eleanor Parker, Tim Henry, and Laurence Naismith. A nephew (Sarrazin) threatens the life of his aunt (Eleanor Parker), who owns dozens of cats.

The Goldwyn Follies (1938)
A musical starring Adolph Menjou, Andrea Leeds, Kenny Baker, The Ritz Brothers, Zorina, Helen Jepson, Bobby Clark, Edgar Bergen and Charlie McCarthy, and hundreds of cats.

The Incredible Journey (1963)
A Disney movie about two dogs and a cat who travel 250 miles in Canada to be with their owners. Starring Emile Genest, John Drainie, Tommy Tweed, and Sandra Scott. The cat's role was played by Syn Cat, personally named by Walt Disney because "he synchronizes so well with everything."

Shadow of the Cat (1961)
A British production starring Barbara Shelley, Andre Morell, William Lucas, Richard Warner, and Freda Jackson. A horror film about a cat that avenges the murder of its owner.

That Darn Cat (1965)
A Disney feature starring Hayley Mills, Dean Jones, Dorothy Provine, Roddy McDowall, Neville Brand, Elsa Lanchester, William Demarest, Frank Gorshin and Ed Wynn. About a cat, played by Syn Cat, that helps an FBI agent (Jones) find a kidnapped woman.

Track of the Cat (1954)
A John Wayne production, starring Robert Mitchum, Teresa Wright, Diana Lynn, Tab Hunter, and Carl "Alfalfa" Switzer. Mitchum tracks down a black panther that is killing his cattle.

The Three Lives of Thomasina (1963)
Based on Paul Gallico's story about an aloof veterinarian, his daughter's fascination with and devotion to her cat, and a woman with special life-giving powers. Starring Patrick McGoohan, Susan Hampshire, Karen Dotrice, and Vincent Winter.

The Tomb of Ligeia (1965)
A British film production based on an Edgar Allen Poe story directed by Roger Corman. About a husband's dead wife who manifests herself as both his new bride and as a cat. Starring Vincent Price, Elizabeth Shepherd, John Westbrook, Richard Johnson, and Derek Francis.

Torture Garden (1968)
A British production starring Jack Palance, Burgess Meredith, Beverly Adams, Peter Cushing, Barbara Ewing, Michael Bryant, and Maurice Denham. An anthology of tales, one of which is about a "diabolical" cat.

A Walk on the Wild Side (1962)
Based on Nelson Algren novel, starring Laurence Harvey, Capucine, Jane Fonda, Anne Baxter, and Barbara Stanwyck.

The Wrong Box (1966)
British comedy based on a story by Robert Louis Stevenson, starring John Mills, Ralph Richardson, Michael Caine, Peter Cook, Dudley Moore, Nanette Newman, Wilfred Lawson, Tony Hancock, and Peter Sellers in a funny cameo role.

"OSCAR" WINNING CATS: PATSY AWARDS

The Patsy awards were instituted in 1951 by the American Humane Society of Los Angeles to acknowledge the contributions of animals in the movies and on television. Patsy, by the way, is an acronym for Picture Animal Top Star Award.

The following are felines who have won the award through the years:

1952 RHUBARB (a.k.a. Orangey)

For its performance in the movie *Rhubarb* starring Ray Milland, Jan Sterling, Gene Lockhart, William Frawley, Elsie Holmes, and Leonard Nimoy. Based on a story by H. Allen Smith, the movie is about a cat that inherits a baseball team. (Rhubarb also played the role of Minerva, the cat owned by Eve Arden's landlord in the 1950s television series *Our Miss Brooks*.)

1959 PYEWACKET

For its performance in the movie *Bell, Book and Candle* starring Kim Novak, James Stewart, and Jack Lemmon; based on the John Van Druten play.

1962 RHUBARB (a.k.a. Orangey)

For its performance as Cat in the movie *Breakfast at Tiffany's* starring Audrey Hepburn, George Peppard, and Mickey Rooney; based on Truman Capote's novella.

Rhubarb, "for his performance as cat in the movie 'Breakfast at Tiffany's'..."

1966 SYN CAT

The Siamese cat in the 1965 Disney movie *That Darn Cat* starring Dean Jones and Hayley Mills; about a cat who helps an FBI agent find a kidnapped woman.

1973 MORRIS

For his popular appearances in 9-Lives cat food commercials

1974 MIDNIGHT

For its regular appearances in the *Mannix* and *Barnaby Jones* television series.

1975 TONTO

For its performance in the movie *Harry and Tonto* starring Art Carney, who won the Oscar that year for Best Supporting Actor.

1977 17

For its performance in the movie *Dr. Shrinker*.

1979 AMBER

For its performance the Disney movie *The Cat From Outer Space* starring Ken Berry, Sandy Duncan, McLean Stevenson, Harry Morgan, Roddy McDowall, and Ronnie Schell. About a cat from another planet who visits earth to get scientists to fix its spaceship.

1986 VARIOUS CATS

For the *Alfred Hitchcock Presents* television series.

MUSICAL CATS

A unique "pipe" organ made of cats was contrived by the Belgians on the occasion of a visit to Brussels by Charles V (1500–1558), then King of Spain and the Holy Roman Empire. Instead of pipes, cats were placed in boxes with their tails pulled through a hole in the back of the box and attached by string to the keyboard. The resulting sound could be called pure "cat-cophony," but it was a novelty act popular enough to tour London and Paris.

Eighteenth-century Italian composer Domenico Scarlatta wrote *Fuga del Gatta* ("Fugue of the Cat").

Giacchino Rossini, a nineteenth-century Italian composer, wrote *Dueto Buffo due Gatti* ("Comic Duet of Two Cats"), which musically depicted two cats joyfully meowing.

Violin strings made of "catgut" are actually made of "sheepgut" or the twisted dry intestines of sheep. (It is also used for stringing tennis racquets and for surgical sutures. The *samisen*, a three-stringed Japanese instrument, was actually made from real "catgut.")

Andrew Lloyd Webber's West End and Broadway musical *Cats* has been running since 1981, making it one of the longest-running musicals of all time. It is based on a short book, *An Old Possum's Book of Practical Cats*, written for children by American poet T. S. Eliot.

THE CAT IN ART

CECILIA BEAUX (1836–1942), *Man with the Cat* (Henry Sturgis Drinker), man sitting in chair with a cat on his lap

GEORGE CALEB BINGHAM (1811–1879), *Fur Traders Descending the Missouri*, two men in a row boat with a cat in the front of the boat

LÉOPOLD LOUIS BOILLY (1727–1775), French artist, mother, daughter, and son petting cat

PIERRE BONNARD (1867–1947), *The White Cat*, stylized portrait of a cat with extra long legs

JEAN-BAPTISTE CHARDIN (1699–1779), *The Ray*, a cat on a table with victuals, including a stingray

LEONARDO DA VINCI (1452–1519), *Madonna with the Cat*

ALEXANDRE DESPORTES (1661–1743), untitled painting of a cat pawing a dish of oysters on the half shell

PAULUS DE VOS (1596–1678), *Cat Fight in a Larder*, five or six cats raiding a kitchen

FRANÇOIS DROUAIS (1727–1775), a young girl holding her cat

THOMAS GAINSBOROUGH (1727–1788), *Studies of a Cat*, sketches of a cat in six different positions

MARGUERITE GÉRARD (1761–1837), *The Cat's Dinner*, a kneeling woman feeding a cat a plate of food

ALBERTO GIACOMETTI (1901–1966), *Cat*, modernistic sculpture of cat

FRANCISCO GOYA (1797–1798), *Trials*, two cats in foreground of a nude male and female in front of a horned beast; *The Dream of Reason Produces Monsters*

JEAN-BAPTISTE GREUZE (1725–1805), *The Ball of Wool*, a cat at the left arm of a girl holding a ball of wool

HIROSHIGE (1797–1858), *Cat at a Window*, a cat looking out of a window, overlooking the city of Edo (now Tokyo); *Cat Washing*

MORRIS HIRSCHFIELD (1872–1996), *Angora Cat*, modernistic painting of a white cat on a chair

WILLIAM HOGARTH (1697–1764), *The Graham Children*, a cat staring at a caged bird; etching, *The First Phase of Cruelty*, stray cats being attacked

NATHANIEL HONE (1718–1784), *Kitty Fisher*, a woman with a cat next to her, gazing at a fishbowl

JOHN HOPPNER (1758–1810), *Boy with his Cat*, a boy in a red jacket hugging his cat

TOMOO INAGAKI, *Cats Making Up*, modern painting of two cats

KUNIYOSHI (1797–1861), studies of various cats for the fifty-three stages of the Tokaido, and a drawing of a group of cats forming the Japanese word for "catfish"

FRANZ VON LENBACK (1836–1904), *Miss Peck*, a woman hugging her cat

EDOUARD MANET (1832–1883), *Olympia*, featuring a black cat

GOTTFRIED MIND (1768–1814), Swiss painter; *Raphael of Cats*, a cat washing itself

PABLO PICASSO (1881–1973), *Le Chat*, sketch of a cat sitting erect

ARTHUR RACKHAM (1867–1939), British illustrator, drawing of girl trying to shake a cat off a small tree

PIERRE-AUGUSTE RENOIR (1841–1919), *Sleeping Girl with Cat*, *Julie Manet with a Cat*, and others

HENRIETTE RONNER (1821–1909), Dutch artist, *Cat's World*, cat and kittens by a globe; *A Turbulent Family*, cat and kittens knocking over a birdcage, and other paintings

HENRI ROUSSEAU (1844–1910), *The Sleeping Gypsy*, a lion next to a sleeping woman

CHARLES SHEELER (1883–1965), *Feline Felicity*, a cat napping in the sun on a ladderback chair

CHARLES SMELDON, Edgar Allan Poe and his cat Catalina

THÉOPHILE STEINLEN (1859–1923), *The Cat and the Ball of Thread*

MARCUS STONE (1840–1921), *There Is Always Another*, a white cat on steps in front of a man and woman

**Henri de Toulouse Lautrec
sketched a cat stalking a mouse.**

HENRI DE TOULOUSE-LAUTREC (1864–1901), *Cat Stalking Mouse*, a sketch of a cat chasing a mouse

M. VERTES (1895–1962), French, color drawing of the writer Colette with two cats

CONELIS VISCHER (1610–1670), *The Big Cat*, drawing of cat, with a mouse behind it

LOUIS WAIN (1860–1939), *Puck*, close-up drawing of a cat

JEAN-ANTOINE WATTEAU (1684–1721), *The Sick Cat*

HARRISON WEIR (1824–1906), British author and illustrator, *Cat and Birds*

More artists who painted cats:

Hieronymous Bosch, Breugel, Alexander Calder, Campagnola, Mary Cassatt, Marc Chagall, Gustave Courbet, George Cruikshank, Honoré Daumier, Delacroix, Gustave Doré, Albrecht Dürer, Foujita, Jean Fragonard, Paul Gaugin, Paul Klee, Hans von Kulmbach, Jean-Baptiste Ordry, Pinturicchio, Reubens, Rembrandt, John Singer Sargent, John Tenniel, Tiepolo, Tintoretto, Titian, Suzanne Valadon, Veronese

3
A Different
Breed of Cat
Cat Breeds and Fascinating
Facts About Them

INTERESTING FACTS ABOUT
SPECIFIC BREEDS

Abyssinian

Based on archaeological documents and mummified remains, many people believe that the Abyssinian is the real ancestor of the domestic cat.

Unlike most breeds of cat, the Abyssinian likes to swim and was once used to retrieve water fowl for hunters.

Abyssinians are very intelligent and can be taught tricks more easily than other breeds.

Abyssinians do not make good apartment pets—they are active and athletic and don't like to be confined.

Famous owners of Abyssinians have included author Tomie de Paola, writer Gladys Taber, columnist Liz Smith, actress Nancy Walker, and actor Christopher Walken.

American Bobtail

This breed originated in Arizona, where the Foster family found a male kitten at the motel in which they were staying. When Yodie, as they named it, matured and mated with Mishi, the family's Siamese cat, several of the kittens had small tails and when they matured they resembled small lynxes.

American Curl

The American Curl is one of the few breeds in which the ears are curled and curved backward.

The breed dates back only to 1981, when a stray black cat with curled-back, hardened ears was discovered by Mr. and Mrs. Ruga of Lakewood, California. Given the name Shulamith, the cat gave birth on December 12, 1981, to four kittens, two of which had curled ears. At the advice of friends, the Rugas entered the cats in shows and received enough acceptance to be officially registered by The International Cat Association (TICA) in 1985 under the name American Curl.

The Balinese breed was named by
a breeder who thought these cats
resembled Balinese dancers.

American Shorthair

The American Shorthair is the WASP of the cat world—it is believed that its ancestors came to America via the Mayflower and early Pilgrim voyages.

American Wirehair

A genetic mutation of the soft-furred American Shorthair, the Wirehair's coat feels rough and prickly because the tips of the primary hairs are bent.

Angora

Angoras originated in Turkey where its capital city, Angora, was changed to Ankara in 1930.

Among the famous people who have owned Angora cats are French writer Honoré de Balzac, Czechoslovakian playwright Karel Capek, French writer Théophile Gautier, singer Whitney Houston, and U.S. President William McKinley.

Balinese

This breed was originally called a longhaired Siamese but a cat breeder renamed it because he thought these cats resembled Balinese dancers.

Bengal

A large spotted cat weighing up to twenty-two pounds, the Bengal is a hybrid of the Leopard Cat found in Asia and the domestic cat, usually an American Shorthair. Although it is not a particularly vocal cat, when it makes sounds, it tends to sound more wild than domestic.

Birman

This breed, not to be confused with the Burmese cat, originated in Burma (now known as Myanmar) where only aristocrats were permitted to own them. They might have become extinct except for the fact that two foreigners, British major Gordon Russell and Auguste Pavie, rescued priests and these sacred cats from their besieged temples in Burma. They were given a pair of this unusual breed as a gift in 1919 when Russell returned to England. The male died en route but the female—pregnant—survived and enabled the breed to survive.

Birmans always have white "gloves" or paws.

Bombay

The Bombay, a cross between a Burmese and a black American Shorthair, is a breed that loves human company and purrs compulsively. Its coat is so smooth, glossy, and black that it has been likened to patent leather. It was named Bombay after the Indian city because it resembled a small version of the Indian black leopard.

When a Bengal cat vocalizes, it sounds
more wild than domestic.

British Shorthair

The British Shorthair breeds are descended from the cats that accompanied Roman soldiers on their conquests of the British Isles.

Burmese

All Burmese cats are descendants of a brown female named Wong Mau, imported to the United States in 1930, and a Siamese male.

A Burmese cat owned by Valerie Gane of Oxfordshire, England, gave birth (by cesarean section) to a record litter of nineteen kittens in 1970. Four were stillborn, and of the remaining kittens, fourteen were male and only one female.

Actresses Victoria Principal and Valerie Bertinelli and her husband, rock singer Eddie Van Halen, have owned Burmese cats.

Burmilla

This relatively new and rare breed of cat is the cross between a lilac-colored Burmese female and a Silver Persian (Chinchilla) male, originally bred in the United Kingdom in the early 1980s.

Calico

A male calico cat is indeed rare but, contrary to popular belief, is not worth a lot of money.

Cornish Rex

A Cornish Rex kitten at birth resembles a baby bat because of its large ears and lean look.

People who are normally allergic to cats usually have no reactions to Cornish Rex cats because they lack the long guard hairs that often cause reactions. (Their hair is very short and wavy.)

At the advice of geneticists, Kallibunker, the first Cornish Rex cat, had to mate with its mother, Serena, in order to continue the new breed. (Because the wavy-hair gene was recessive, Kallibunker had to mate with another cat carrying the gene and its mother was the only known carrier of the gene.) The litter produced two tomcats: one died before maturity and the other was accidentally sterilized—threatening extinction of the young breed. However, one male was left from another litter and crossed with British Shorthairs and Burmese and saved the breed.

Devon Rex

The Devon Rex is a playful cat that wags its tail like a dog and has curly hair, giving it the nickname the "poodle cat."

Egyptian Mau

A spotted breed that originated in Egypt, the Mau is believed to be descended from the cat worshiped thousands of years ago. Its forehead has a scarab-shaped pattern—the scarab beetle being a sacred symbol in Egyptian culture. The word mau, by the way, was the ancient Egyptian word for "cat" and was an onomatopoeic word for "meow."

Havana Brown

Contrary to its name, this chestnut-brown cat with Siamese lineage was bred in England, not Cuba. It was so named because its color resembled the rich brown of the tobacco in Cuban cigars.

Himalayan

Himalayan cats tend to have larger litters than most other breeds.

Regardless of coat color, Himalayans have bright sapphire-blue eyes.

Himalayans are relatively loyal cats and will follow their owners around the house.

The first American-bred Himalayan was born at the Harvard Medical School in 1935.

Famous owners of Himalayans include actresses Morgan Fairchild, Loni Anderson, and Donna Mills, and television talk show host Regis Philbin.

Japanese Bobtail

The tail of the Japanese Bobtail is uniquely short and fluffy like a pompom.

When seated, a Japanese Bobtail occasionally raises one of its front paws, a pose considered to produce good luck.

The Mi-Ke or Calico variety of Japanese Bobtail is considered to be especially lucky.

The Japanese Bobtail is credited with once saving Japan's silk industry by reducing the rodent population that was feeding on the valuable silkworms.

Korat

Korats originated in the province of Korat in Thailand, where they are referred to as Si-Sawat (good fortune). Thai brides are traditionally given a pair of Korats for good luck in their marriages.

Korat kittens have yellow or amber eyes until they are two years old, at which time their eyes turn green.

People normally allergic to cats do not have reactions to Korats because petting them does not loosen their fur.

Maine Coon

The Maine Coon is the oldest American cat breed, dating back to the seventeenth century, when Angoras brought by British sailors mated with the cats roaming the Maine woods.

Originally bred on farms and needing lots of territory, the Maine Coon cat is a large breed, averaging between fifteen and twenty pounds.

Maine Coons often sleep in unusual places.

Maine Coons make an unusual chirping sound.

Author Roger Caras, actress Bo Derek, and science fiction author James Gunn are among Maine Coon owners.

Manx

The only tailless domestic cat is the Manx (and longhaired Manx, known as the Cymric), which has a dimple where its tail would normally be. (It is nicknamed a "Rumpy" unless it has a rudimentary tail—one to three caudal bones—in which case it is a "Stumpy.")

The Manx's hind legs are longer than its forelegs, giving it a rabbit-like gait.

The Isle of Man, a British possession where the breed developed, issued a coin in 1971 that featured a Manx cat on the reverse side (and Queen Elizabeth II on the other side).

The Manx is not a true-breeding cat. When an egg containing the Manx gene is fertilized by a sperm containing a Manx gene, the resulting kittens usually die in the uterus. The breed survives only when one sex gene is carrying the Manx gene, so they are usually mated with American, British, and European shorthairs.

Munchkin

Yes, there really is a new breed of cat named the Munchkin, which is often called the "dachshund" of cats because it has short legs. The kitten-like cat descended from a black female named Blackberry in Louisiana, where most of the registered Munchkins come from.

Ocicat

A combination of an Abyssinian and Siamese, this breed was named by the daughter of the breeder, Virginia Daly, who thought that the spotted kitten (Tonga) looked like an ocelot.

Persian

The Persian is the most popular pure breed cat, according to the Cat Fancy Association.

Blue-eyed White Persian cats tend to be deaf.

Blue-Cream Persians and Calico Persians are usually females.

White Persians with one orange eye and one blue eye are occasionally the product of interbreeding between orange-eyed and blue-eyed types. (If the cat is deaf in one ear, it is usually the ear closest to the blue eye.)

The Tortoiseshell Persian is very expensive because it is difficult to breed.

Some cat associations recognize 148 variations of hair coats in the Persian breed.

Persian are a popular breed owned by famous people, including actors Willie Aames, Loni Anderson, Ed Asner, Catherine Bach, Richard Crenna, Bo Derek, Erik Estrada, Morgan Fairchild, Fannie Flagg, Joan Fontaine, Tony Geary, Lisa Hartman, Marty Ingels, Shirley Jones, Marilyn Monroe, Clayton Moore; writers Albert Payson Terhune, F. Scott and Zelda Fitzgerald, Raymond Chandler, Mark Twain, and Matthew Arnold; and singers Mariah Carey, Whitney Houston, Aaron Neville, and Frankie Valli. Other Persian owners include Yoko Ono, nurse Florence Nightingale, physician Erasmus Darwin, and heiress/arts patron Peggy Guggenheim.

Ragdoll

Originating in California in the 1960s, the Ragdoll is a "laid-back" cat—it can relax so much that it appears as inanimate as a ragdoll, hence its name.

The Ragdoll appears to be relatively insensitive to pain.

The Ragdoll does not attain its full size until the age of four, and is exceptionally large. An average male weighs between fifteen and twenty pounds, comparable in size to a Maine Coon.

Russian Blue

Once known as a Maltese, an Archangel, a Spanish Blue, and American Blue, the Russian Blue is a quiet, shy cat that does not like to wander away from home. It is a good cat for a single person because it tends to attach itself only to one person.

Scottish Fold

The Scottish Fold, like a seal, appears to have no ears but, in fact, has ears that are folded tightly against the side of its head.

Scottish Folds should not be interbred because the offspring are usually born with bone disorders. They are mated with American and British Shorthairs.

Siamese

The Siamese is the most popular shorthaired breed in the U.S., according to the Cat Fancy Association.

When a female Siamese cat mates with a common tomcat, the offspring resembles the tomcat, not the mother.

Originating in California in the 1960s,
the Ragdoll is a "laid back" cat.

Siamese (and Himalayan) cats tend to have larger litters than most other breeds.

Siamese cats tend to get jealous and don't like competition.

When unhappy, Siamese cats emit louder sounds than most cats.

Siamese cats were introduced in England when King Chulalongkorn of Siam (now Thailand) gave Owen Gould, the retiring British consul general in Bangkok, a pair of Siamese cats named Pho and Mia. This gift was a great honor because traditionally only royalty was permitted to own Siamese cats.

The first Siamese cat ever exhibited in England was oddly named Mrs. Poodles.

Siamese cats are prone to a gene-linked eyesight problem which gives them reduced binocular vision and blurred vision, causing them to squint.

The original British standards for the Siamese breed called for crossed eyes and a kinked tail, which are now considered genetic defects. Legend has it, however, that Siamese princesses preferred those cats with kinked tails so before bathing they could hang their rings and necklaces on the cats' tails.

Among famous Siamese owners have been singer Roberta Flack and actors Jack Albertson, Ed Asner, Tallulah Bankhead, Jamie Lyn Bauer, Richard Burton, Kim Cattrall, James Dean, Linda Evans, Erroll Flynn, Eva Gabor, Greer Garson, Gertrude Lawrence, Vivien Leigh, James and Pamela Mason, Vincent Price, Miranda Richardson, Tanya Roberts, Shelley Smith, Cybill Shepherd, and Elizabeth Taylor. Writers who have owned Siamese cats include Roger Caras, Paul Gallico, James Gunn, Frances and Richard Lockridge, and Gladys Taber. The families of U. S. presidents Gerald R. Ford, Rutherford B. Hayes, Lyndon B. Johnson, and Jimmy Carter have owned Siamese cats, as did British prime minister Harold Wilson.

Singapura

Named after the city of Singapore where the breed originated, Singapuras are also known as "Drain Cats" because they roam wild and often live in water drains and sewers in cities.

Usually weighing no more than six pounds, the Singapura is the smallest breed of domestic cat.

The most valuable cat in the world, according to the Guinness Book of World Records, was a Singapura named Bull. Its owner was offered $10,000 for the special cat but turned the offer down.

Somali

The Somali breed is essentially a longhaired Abyssinian with a fox-like tail. It looks like a wild cat, prefers the outdoors, and is an excellent hunter.

Sphinx

The Sphinx (originally bred in Canada, not Egypt) is the only breed of cat that lacks fur. Although it appears to be totally hairless, it has a coat of short, fine down and has some sparse hair on its face, ears, legs, and tail. The skin feels like suede or chamois. (The feel of it has been likened to a "suede hot-water bottle.")

Although it is a friendly breed, the Sphinx does not like to be handled.

Because it lacks a thick coat of hair, the Sphinx sweats, unlike other breeds. It should be sponged regularly and should not be exposed to changes in temperature.

Tabby

The Tabby cat (not a breed but a type of coat) was named after the Attabiya district in Bagdad, Iraq, where weavers used a pattern of silk called tabbi, which strongly resembled the cat's markings.

The Tabby pattern is attributed to the "agouti" gene, which is responsible for creating alternate light and dark bands on each hair.

Tonkinese

Originally called a Golden Siamese, the Tonkinese is a cross between a Burmese and a Siamese. The breed's eye color varies from turquoise to aquamarine, a blend of the Burmese gold and Siamese blue.

Tortoiseshell

Due to a sex-linked gene, tortoiseshell cats (not a breed but a type of coloration) are almost always female. A male tortoise-shell is extremely rare and is invariably infertile.

Turkish

The British Turkish cat, like the Abyssinian, takes to water and enjoys swimming.

MOST POPULAR BREEDS
IN RANK ORDER

The Cat Fancy Association is the largest official registering body of pedigreed cats in the U.S. The following are the breeds in rank order by number of registered cats in that breed:

1. Persian
2. Maine Coon Cat
3. Siamese
4. Abyssinian
5. Exotic
6. Scottish Fold
7. Oriental Shorthair
8. American Shorthair
9. Birman
10. Burmese
11. Cornish Rex
12. Tonkinese
13. Ocicat
14. Manx (and Cymric)
15. Somali
16. Devon Rex
17. Russian Blue
18. Colorpoint Shorthair
19. British Shorthair
20. Japanese Bobtail
21. Ragdoll
22. Balinese
23. Egyptian Mau
24. Norwegian Forest Cat
25. Chartreux
26. American Curl
27. Javanese
28. Turkish Angora
29. Korat
30. Bombay
31. Singapura
32. Havana Brown
33. American Wirehair
34. Turkish Van
35. Oriental Longhair
36. Selkirk Rex
37. European Burmese

WILD CATS: LARGE AND SMALL

Other than size, the main difference between domestic cats and wild cats is the latter's ability to roar. All cats have hyoid bones along the side of their throats, which affects sounds produced by the larynx, but wild cats' hyoid bones contain cartilage. This flexible cartilage enables the larynx to expand more and therefore produce loud roars instead of meek meows.

A group of lions is called a pride of lions but a group of wild cats is sometimes referred to as a "doubt of cats" or a "destruction of cats."

Wild cats have existed on most continents but have been surprisingly absent in Australia, although occasional sightings have been claimed.

African Wild Cat

The African wild cat (*Felis silvestris libyca*) is the closest relative and probable ancestor of the domestic cat.

Despite its name, the African wild cat is found on Mallorca, Corsica, Sardinia, Sicily, Crete, and Israel—in addition to Morocco and Tunisia, only the latter two being in Africa.

Black-footed Cat

One of the smallest of wild cats, the Black-footed cat (*Felis nigripes*) weighs no more than five and a half pounds but can roar as loud as a tiger, albeit at a higher octave. It is found in the deserts of Namibia, Botswana, and South Africa.

Bobcat

A wild bobcat occasionally will mate with a domestic cat but the resulting offspring usually die.

Cheetah

The cheetah is the fastest-running land animal—it reaches sixty-five to seventy miles per hour but can only sustain the speed for 200- to 300-yard sprints. It can reach a speed of forty-five miles per hour in only two seconds and hit seventy miles per hour in three seconds.

Cheetahs have several canine characteristics. They have hard footpads and their claws are not retractable. Cheetahs also make sounds that resemble barks more than roars or meows.

Their unique longitudinal footpads (analogous to tire treads) enable Cheetahs to get superior traction and excellent ability to make quick turns.

Cheetahs are easily tamed and have been so since 1500 B.C., in the days of the Egyptian pharaohs, who used them and trained dogs on their hunting expeditions. In India cheetahs were also used for hunting.

The Medicis of Florence owned cheetahs and hunted with them. In fact, the cheetah was a Medici family symbol.

Civet Cat

The African civet cat is the source of musk used in many perfumes. The name civet is derived from the Arabic word *zubad*, which referred to the perfume of this particular cat.

Cougar

The cougar, puma, mountain lion, and panther are all names for the same animal (*Felis concolor*).

The cougar has the largest range of any native New World mammal. It can be found from British Columbia, Canada, to the southern tip of South America.

Iriomote

The Iriomote cat (*Felis iriomotensis*) is so rare that it is found in only one area—on Iriomote, an island and Japanese possession off Taiwan.

Jaguar

The word "jaguar" is from the Tupi Indian word *jaguara*, which means "he who strikes down his prey in a single bound."

In fact, jaguars are noteworthy for the way they attack their prey. It is the only cat that doesn't bite the throat—it bites the skull of its prey.

Jungle Cat

The Jungle cat (*Felis chaus*), contrary to its name, does not live in the jungle. It inhabits woods, reedy areas near rivers, swamps, marshes, and lakes. It is found in the deltas of the Nile and Volga rivers, and in China, India, Turkestan, and the Indo-China region.

Leopard

The leopard has the largest range of any cat. It inhabits most of Africa and Asia, in terrains as varied as tropical rain forests and the high altitudes of the Himalayas.

Liger

The cross between a male lion and female tiger.

Lion

Lions are the only wild cats that travel in family groups (prides), and are the most social of wild cats.

While female lions do most of the hunting, they allow the males to eat the kill before they and the cubs eat.

Egyptian pharaoh Ramses II kept a pet lion named Antamnekht, which sometimes accompanied him in battle.

Lions have been known to go ten days without drinking water.

Lions, like domestic cats, are inveterate sleepers and usually spend about twenty hours a day snoozing and resting.

When male lions are around three years old, they are driven out of their pride by older, dominant males, to fend for themselves until they become old and strong enough to dominate a new pride.

During the mating process, a lioness will initiate mating with a male and may have sexual intercourse every fifteen minutes for five or six hours. A female lion in heat has been known to copulate as often as 150 times in fifty-five hours. The actual sex act takes less than twenty seconds, and sometimes just a few seconds. During the rite, the lioness circles the male, flicks her tail at his face, gives off her scent, and prances away growling— soon to be agreeably mounted by the male. After intercourse, the female gets belligerent and discourages the male, but soon comes back to initiate intercourse again.

When an adult male takes over a new pride, it will often kill the cubs sired by other males. Biologically, the male is interested in propagating its own genes, and makes a bad "stepfather."

Lions can eat sixty pounds of meat during a single feeding.

Lions make most of their kills at night. Daytime attempts make better footage for television nature shows, but lions are successful only 5 percent of the time during the day.

Litigon

A cross between an Indian male lion and a female tigon (the cross between a male tiger and female lion), litigons are on display at the Alipore Zoological Gardens in Calcutta, India.

Rusty Spotted Cat

The Rusty Spotted Cat of India and Ceylon almost never weighs more than three pounds, making it the smallest wild cat in the world. It is less than half the weight of the average domestic cat. It averages sixteen inches in length, not counting its tail, or about three inches shorter than the average domestic cat.

Sand Cat

The Sand cat (*Felis margarita*) or Margueritte's cat, found in the Sahara and Arabian deserts, rarely drinks water but survives on the liquids found in its prey (reptiles, birds, rodents, and locusts).

The footpads of the Sand cat are very furry, which helps it walk on the hot desert sand.

Snow Leopard

Contrary to its name, the snow leopard, a protected species, lives below the snow line in the Himalayas and the mountains of northern Pakistan, China, and Mongolia. However, it does traverse snowy terrain especially if, by doing so, it finds prey.

The going price for a coat made of Snow Leopard fur is $60,000 on the black market. (The original three pelts needed to make the coat probably earned the original poachers less than $1,000—with the rest of the money going to middlemen, coat makers, and dealers.)

Tarai

The Tarai, or fishing cat, is the only wild cat that almost exclusively feeds on fish and other freshwater aquatic prey, which it catches in mangrove swamps and in rivers. Found mostly in China, Sri Lanka, and India, the fishing cat occasionally eats small mammals and snakes when the fishing is not good.

Tiger

Although lions are known as "The King of the Beasts," tigers tend to be the larger animal. A Siberian tiger can measure over twelve feet in length and weigh about 600 pounds.

Tigers copulate four to twenty times a day, for up to three weeks.

A Bengal tiger consumes about three tons of meat per year, equivalent to the meat from about seventy axis deer. (Three tons of meat is equal to about sixteen and a half pounds per day.)

Unlike domestic and most wild cats, tigers are excellent swimmers and comfortably cross rivers and take dips in lakes.

Some rare Bengal tigers have black and white coloration. They trace back to a white tiger named Bohan, found as a cub over forty years ago.

Tigon

A cross between a male tiger and female lion.

The Tarai, or fishing cat, occasionally
eats small mammals and snakes when
the fishing is not good.

THE MOST POPULAR NAMES
FOR CATS

In the U.S. the top names for female cats in order of popularity are Samantha, Misty, Patches, Cali, Calico, Muffin, Angel, Angela, Ginger, Tiger, Tigger, Princess, Punkin, and Pumpkin.

The top names for male cats are Tiger, Tigger, Smokey, Pepper, Max, Maxwell, Simon, Snoopy, Morris, Mickey, Rusty, Rusti, Boots, and Bootsie.

The most popular names of British cats in rank order are Sooty, Smokie, Brandy, Fluffy, Tiger, Tibbie, Tiggie, Tom, Kitty, Sam, Sandy, Tinker, Blackie, Susie, Toby, Whisky, Ginger, Lucy, Tim, Tiny, Charlie, Lucky, Rusty, Snowy, Candy, Cat, Flossie, Mitzi, Puss, Sally, Sukie, Tammy, Bumble, Cindy, Daisy, Dusty, Fred, Frisky, Honey, Jerry, Katie, Kizzy, Mickey, Nelson, Oliver, Penny, Pepper, Pickles, Purdy, Sammy, Scamp, Shandy, Sherry, Simon, Tabitha, Topsy, and Twiggy.

Miscellaneous

THE FAMOUS CATS OF T. S. ELIOT

T. S. Eliot's *Old Possum's Book of Practical Cats*, on which the Broadway musical *Cats* is based, is a celebration of cats and the naming of them. Here are Eliot's cats in his writings and his descriptions of them:

Peter, Augustus, Alonzo, James, Victor, Jonathan, George and Bill Bailey had "sensible everyday names." Plato, Admetus, Electra, and Demeter were "fancier names" but were also "sensible everyday names."

Names that "never belong to more than one cat" are Munkustrap, Quaxo, Coricopat, Bombalurina, and Jellylorum.

Asparagus, also known as Gus, was a "Theatre Cat" and a "Star of the highest degree." He once received seven cat-calls.

Bustopher Jones was a fat black "Cat About Town" who belonged to "eight or nine clubs" and wore "well-cut trousers" and white spats.

Griddlebone was enraptured by Growltiger's "manly baritone," the latter being the "roughest cat" and "Terror of the Thames." Grumbuskin was a "bucko mate" of Growltiger. Tumblebrutus was Growltiger's "bosun" cat.

Jennyanydots, the "Gumbie Cat," had a tabby coat and "tiger stripes and leopard spots."

Macavity, a tall, thin ginger cat, was the "Napoleon Crime" who had "broken every human law."

Mr. Mistoffelees was the tiny, black "Original Conjuring Cat," who produced "seven kittens right out of a hat."

Morgan was the ex-pirate with a kind heart.

Rumpelteazer and Mungojerrie were "quick-change comedians" and "highly efficient cat-burglars."

Old Deuteronomy was an old cat who "lived many lives" and "buried many wives."

Great Rumpus Cat was a fierce cat.

Rum Tum Tugger was a "Curious Cat."

Skimbleshanks was the "Railway Cat" that was always "fresh and bright," even in the middle of the night.

Other felines owned by T. S. Eliot include Carbucketty, Cassandra, Etcetera, Grizabella, Pouncival, Sillabub, and Tantomile.

CAT OWNERS AND OWNERSHIP

The United States has the largest cat population in the world. There are about 64,000,000 cats in the U.S.! About one-fourth of American households own cats.

Cat ownership in various countries by percent of household ownership is:

Australia (32 percent)

Canada (27 percent)

U.S.A. (26 percent)

Austria (23 percent)

France (22 percent)

Netherlands (20 percent)

Norway (20 percent)

Switzerland (20 percent)

Belgium (19 percent)

United Kingdom (19 percent)

Denmark (16 percent)

Finland (16 percent)

Italy (16 percent)

Sweden (15 percent)

West Germany (9 percent)

Japan (6 percent)

Cat owners, according to psychologist David Greene, tend "to be independent, freedom-loving individuals, self-reliant and slightly aloof from the rest of humanity." He also notes that cat owners prefer "not to involve themselves too deeply in the lives of their fellows."

Dog owners, on the other hand, "tend to be more dependent on others and want to involve themselves in the lives and problems of those around them." Greene added, "They are more likely to be assertive and to confront problems head-on, standing their ground and fighting when challenged." Soldiers and presidents tend to be dog owners. Artists and writers tend to be cat owners. Cat lovers are more apt to be female. Cat haters tend to be males, specifically tyrants and dictatorial types. Greene also noted that cat owners are more likely to have drawings and figurines of cats in their homes than dog owners have of dogs in their homes.

A single person is less likely to own a cat than a married couple. About this phenomenon, psychologist David Greene believes, as do many others, that "cats . . . can become a substitute child, evoking feelings which would otherwise be aroused by human infants." California researchers Drs. Robert and Aline Kidd found that only 30 percent of cat owners said that they liked young children versus 48 percent for dog owners, suggesting that some cat owners just don't want children.

West Coast residents are more apt to own a cat than East Coast residents or, for that matter, people from anywhere else in the U.S.

FAT CATS

Brownie and Hellcat, cats owned by Dr. William Grier of San Diego, California, inherited $415,000 when Grier died in 1963.

French harpist Madame Dupuis left a large part of her estate in 1678 to her cats, and to a sister and a niece who were asked to take care of the cats. The will stipulated that if the sister and niece died, thirty sous a week would be spent on the cats "in order that they may live well."

An eighteen-pound white alley cat named Charlie Chan inherited an estate worth $250,000 when its owner Grace Alma Patterson of Joplin, Missouri, died in 1978.

In 1991 a pair of Burmese cats named Damon and Pythias inherited a $750,000 New York co-op apartment on Fifth Avenue after their owner Terry Krumholz died.

A cat named Cyrus inherited an $850,000 mansion in Bridgeport, Connecticut, in 1992 when its owner, Beatrice Farrington, passed away.

A show biz cat named Nicodemus, a snowy-white Persian, earned a lot of money in the 1960s in Revlon commercials and appearances on television shows such as *Captain Kangaroo*, *Play Your Hunch*, the *Today* show, and others.

A pair of Burmese cats named Damon and Pythias inherited a Fifth Avenue apartment.

Many cats benefited from the benevolence of a British bachelor named Ben Rea. A notorious "tightwad" in his lifetime, Rea died in 1990 at the age of eighty-two and left his entire estate, valued at $14 million, to three charities that cared for stray cats. He left nary a farthing to his relatives or loyal housekeeper of forty years. French cats similarly benefited when Lucien and Marcelle Bourdon donated $60 million to cat-oriented charities.

Morris the Cat, spokescat in the 9-Lives canned cat food commercials, has earned millions of dollars in residuals since he debuted in the early 1970s.

The original Morris's real name was Lucky and lucky he was. He was discovered not at Schwab's drugstore but at the Hinsdale, Illinois, Humane Society shelter by animal trainer Bob Martwick, who was looking for a cat to appear in television commercials. Like many movie and TV stars, Lucky was re-named to give him "some dignity and prestige." The name Morris was selected because it was close to the "mmmrrrsss" sound that cats made. Morris became world famous as the spokescat for 9-Lives cat food and won the Patsy award in 1973.

EGYPT AND CATS

The *Egyptian Book of the Dead* referred to the "great cat at the pool of the Persea in Heliopolis." The cat is a symbol for the sun god Osiris or Re who overpowers a serpent (Set or Apophis), the ruler of darkness.

Ancient Egyptian family members shaved off their eyebrows when mourning the death of their cats. (When a family dog died, they shaved off all body hair.)

In a battle between the Egyptians and Persians in 500 B.C., the Persians cleverly used cats as shields—and the Egyptians, who venerated cats, surrendered rather than risk harm to the cats.

In Egypt in 1890 over 300,000 mummified cats (plus mice!) were discovered by archaeologists in huge cat cemeteries. Not considered archaeologically important at the time, the twenty-four tons of history were shipped to England and ground up for use as fertilizer.

CATS AND THE LAW

Saint Ives, the eleventh-century patron saint of lawyers, is shown with a cat, the symbol of justice.

In ancient Egypt, exporting cats was prohibited.

During the reign of King Howell the Good in tenth-century Wales, laws dictated the worth of cats. A kitten was worth a penny, two pence after it made its first kill, and four pence after its fourth kill. Buyers of under-performing cats, such as poor mousers, were entitled to refunds. People who stole or killed cats were fined.

In many U.S. cities it is illegal to bury a cat in your backyard.

Declawing a cat is illegal in the United Kingdom.

U.S. President Ronald Reagan, while governor of California, signed a bill that outlawed kicking cats.

The state Legislature of Illinois almost passed a law in 1949 forbidding cats to leave their owners' property, but Governor Adlai Stevenson vetoed the bill. In making the decision, Stevenson said that it is "the nature of cats to do a certain amount of unescorted roaming," and acknowledged that "cats perform useful services, particularly in rural areas, in combating rodents—work they necessarily perform alone and without regard for property lines."

FELINE FOREIGN EXPRESSIONS AND IDIOMS

FRENCH "chat"

>   "*Appeler un chat un chat*"
>> To call a cat a cat (To call a spade a spade)

>   "*N'eveillez pas le chat qui dort.*"
>> Don't wake a sleeping cat. (Let sleeping dogs lie.)

>   "*C'est mal acheter de chat en sac.*"
>> It's a bad thing to buy a cat in a bag.

ITALIAN "gatto"

>   "*Gatta ci cova.*"
>> There's something fishy going on; I smell a rat.

>   "*Non fu mai cacciator gatto che miagola.*"
>> A cat who meows is not a good hunter.

>   "*Quando non c'è il gatto i topi ballano.*"
>> When the cat's away, the mice will play.

>   "*Tanto va la gatta al lardo che ci lascia lo zampino.*"
>> The pitcher went to the well once too often.

>   "*Avere altre gatte da pelare*"
>> to have other fish to fry

>   "*Aver una gatta da pelare*"
>> to get in a fix; to have a hard nut to crack

>   "*Fare la gatta morta*"
>> to be a hypocrite; to play up to

"*Quando non c'è il gatto i topi ballano.*"
When the cat's away, the mice will play.

"La gatta nel sacco"
  a pig in a poke

"Quattro gatti"
  only a few people

LATIN "cattus"

"Ad cuius veniat scit catus lingere barbaram."
  The cat knows whose beard she licks.

SPANISH "gato"

"De noche todos los gatos son pardos."
  All cats are alike in the dark. Literally: At night all cats
  are gray.

"Los amores del gato riñendo entraran."
  A cat's amorous activities begin with a display of teeth.

"Hay muchos modos de matar pulgas."
  There are more ways than one to skin a cat. Literally:
  There are many ways to kill fleas.

CATS IN PROVERBS AND OTHER SAYINGS

"All cats are gray in the dark."

VARIOUS

"Better be the head of a cat than the tail of a lion."

ENGLISH

"A blind cat catches only a dead rat."

CHINESE

"Can the cat help it if the maid is a fool?"

UNKNOWN

"A cat always eats fish from the tail."

ESTONIAN

"The cat always leaves a mark on his friend."

SPANISH

"A cat bitten once by a snake dreads even rope."

ARABIC

"The cat does not catch mice for God."

INDIAN

"The cat dreams of garbage."

HINDI

"The cat has nine lives—three for playing, three for straying, and three for staying."

UNKNOWN

"A cat in the grass is a tiger in the jungle."
ENGLISH

"A cat in mittens catches no mice."
UNKNOWN

"A cat is hungry when a crust contents her."
UNKNOWN

"A cat is a lion to a mouse."
ALBANIAN

"The cat is a lion in a jungle of small bushes."
ENGLISH

"The cat knows whose beard he licks."
LATIN

"The cat knows whose lips she licks."
LATIN

"The cat laps the moonbeams in the bowl of water,
thinking them to be milk."
HINDI

"The cat loves fish, but hates wet feet."
ITALIAN

"A cat may go to a monastery, but she still remains a cat."
ETHIOPIAN

"The cat shuts its eyes when it steals cream."
ENGLISH

"A cat that is always crying catches no mice."
ARABIC

"A cat that is locked up may change into a lion."

DUTCH

"A cat that meweth loudly catcheth few mice."

DUTCH

"A cat that meows too much catches few mice."

VARIATION OF ABOVE

"The cat who scratches, scratches for himself."

RUSSIAN

"A cat with a straw tail keeps away from the fire."

ENGLISH

"A cat with a straw tail shouldn't sit with her
back to the fire."

VARIATION OF ABOVE

"The cat that does not catch mice, and the man who
does not like to talk, will both go hungry."

CZECH

"Cats and women are said to have
been made on the same day."

GERMAN

"Cats are everywhere at home where one feeds them."

GERMAN

"The cat is saint when there are no mice around."

JAPANESE

"A dog's tongue has nine healings;
a cat's claw has snake's poison."

ESTONIAN

"After eating nine hundred rats, the cat is
now going on a pilgrimage."

HINDI

"A girl without a needle is like a cat without a claw."

ESTONIAN

"A good cat deserves a good rat."

FRENCH

"A house without either a cat or a dog
is the house of a scoundrel."

PORTUGUESE

"A lame cat is better than a swift horse when
rats infest the palace."

CHINESE

"A man who loves cats will marry an immoral woman."

FRENCH

"All women and cats are black in darkness."

BOSNIAN

"An old cat will not burn himself."

IRISH

"At home an elephant, abroad a cat."

TAMIL

"Beware of people who dislike cats."

IRISH

"The borrowed cat catches no mice."

JAPANESE

"A man who loves cats will marry
an immoral woman."

"The cat who frightens the mice away is as
good as the cat that eats them."

GERMAN

"Curiosity killed the cat; satisfaction brought it back."

ENGLISH

"Don't wake a sleeping cat."

ITALIAN

"During his lifetime, a good Hindu must
feed at least one cat."

HINDI

"During the cat's harvest hens are deaf."

DUTCH

"Even mice may bite dead cats."

GERMAN

"Every cat is honest when the meat's put
away in the larder."

UNKNOWN

"For the sake of the grease, the cat licks the candlestick."

DUTCH

"The four fortunes of the cat: the housewife's error,
walking without care, no water in milk,
and sight at night as well as by day."

IRISH

"Give the servant good food, and the cat will yield
more milk and the cat will drink less."

SWEDISH

"Go like a dog; come like a cat."
HINDI

"The greedy cat makes the servant girl watchful."
FRENCH

"Happy owner, happy cat. Indifferent owner, reclusive cat."
CHINESE

"He who denies the cat skimmed milk must
give the mouse cream."
RUSSIAN

"He who is a little cat outside is a little dog at home."
ESTONIAN

"He who will not feed his cat, let him feed mice."
WELSH

"House without hound, cat, or child, house
without love or affection."
IRISH

"If the cat had a churn, her paw would often be in it."
IRISH

"If you do not rear cats, you will raise mice."
BULGARIAN

"If you leave the kitchen door open, don't blame
the cat for stealing meat."
VARIOUS

"If you want to know what a tiger is like, look at a cat."
HINDI

"I gave an order to the cat, and the cat gave it to its tail."

CHINESE

"It takes a good many mice to kill a cat."

DANISH

"It is a brave bird that makes its nest in the cat's ear."

HINDI

"The man who goes to law often loses an ox to win a cat."

ROMANIAN

"No one will lift the cat's tail unless the cat itself does."

FINNISH

"Old cats mean young mice."

ITALIAN

"The rat stops still when the eyes of the cat shine."

MADAGASCAN

"A scalded cat dreads even cold water."

FRENCH AND SPANISH

"Singing cats and whistling girls will come to a bad end."

ENGLISH

"The sleeping cat doesn't catch a mouse."

SPANISH

"They that ever mind the world to win must have a black cat, a howling dog, and a crowing hen."

UNKNOWN

"Those who do not like cats will not get handsome mates."

DUTCH

"Though the cat winks a while, yet sure he is not blind."

"The three most pleasant things: a cat's kitten,
a goat's kid, and a young widow-woman."
IRISH

"Three pairs that never agree: two married women
in the same house, two cats with one mouse, and
two bachelors after one young woman."
IRISH

"A timid cat makes a bold mouse."
SCOTTISH

"To kiss a black cat will make one fat.
To kiss a white cat will make one lean."
UNKNOWN

"To live long, eat like a cat, drink like a dog."
GERMAN

"Touch not the cat but with a glove."
THE MOTTO OF THE MACINTOSH CLAN OF SCOTLAND

"What would a young cat do but eat mice?"
IRISH

"When cat and mouse agree, the farmer has no chance."
ENGLISH

"When the cat's away the mice will play."
VARIOUS

"When the cat washes her face, company is coming."
UNKNOWN

"When the mouse laughs at the cat, there is a hole nearby."

NIGERIAN

"When the cat mourns the mouse,
you need not take her seriously.

JAPAN

"When you have trodden on the cat,
what help is it to stroke her back?"

SWISS-GERMAN

"Whenever a rat teases a cat, he is leaning against a hole."

LIBERIAN

"Wherever the mice laugh at the cat,
there you will find a hole."

PORTUGUESE

"Who can forbid to a cat the top of
the oven, or a boy to a girl."

LIVONIAN

"Who doesn't feed the cat feeds the mice."

SERBIAN

"Who saves, saves for the cat."

ITALIAN

"Whoever has never seen a tiger, let him look at
a cat, and whoever has never seen a robber,
let him look at a butcher."

HINDUSTANI

"You won't get a cat but its skin."

IRISH

FAMOUS QUOTATIONS
ABOUT CATS

"Cruel, but composed and bland,
Dumb, inscrutable and grand,
So Tiberius might have sat,
Had Tiberius been a cat."

MATTHEW ARNOLD, "POOR MATTHIAS"

"Both ardent lovers and austere scholars, when
once they come to the years of discretion, love cats, so
strong and gentle, the pride of the household, who like
them are sensitive to the cold, and sedentary."

CHARLES BAUDELAIRE

"I love cats. I even think we have one at home."

EDWARD BURLINGAME

"Those who will play with cats must
expect to be scratched."

MIGUEL DE CERVANTES

"The cat lives alone. He has no need of society. He
obeys only when he wishes, he pretends to sleep the
better to see, and scratches everything he can scratch."

CHATEAUBRIAND

"I love cats because I love my home, and after a
while they become its visible soul."

JEAN COCTEAU

"By associating with the cat, one only risks
becoming richer."

COLETTE

"Our perfect companions never have fewer than four feet."

COLETTE

"A poet's cat, sedate and grave
As a poet well could wish to have . . ."

WILLIAM COWPER

"To respect the cat is the beginning of the aesthetic sense."

ERASMUS DARWIN

"Cats instinctively know the precise moment their
owners will awaken . . . then they awaken
them ten minutes earlier."

JIM DAVIS

"Some people say that cats are sneaky, evil, and cruel.
True, and they have many other fine qualities as well."

MISSY DIZICK, *Dogs Are Better Than Cats*

"What's virtue in a man can't be vice in a cat."
MARY ABIGAIL DODGE

"I'm not one o' those as can see the cat i' the dairy, an'
wonder what she's come after."
GEORGE ELIOT, *Adam Bede*

"The cat: an animal that's so unpredictable, you can never
tell in advance how it will ignore you the next time."
EVAN ESAR

"A creature that never cries over spilt milk: a cat."
EVAN ESAR

"God has created the cat to give man
the pleasure of caressing the tiger."
THÉOPHILE GAUTIER

"It is no easy task to win the friendship of a cat.
He is a philosopher, sedate, tranquil, a creature of habit,
a lover of decency and order. He does not bestow his
regard lightly, and, though he may consent to be
your companion, he will never be your slave."
THÉOPHILE GAUTIER

"Life will go on forever
With all that a cat can wish
Warmth, and the glad procession
Of fish and milk and fish."

ALEXANDER GRAY, "ON A CAT AGING"

"What female heart can gold despise
What cat's averse to fish?"

THOMAS GRAY, "ODE ON THE DEATH OF A CAT"

"Her purrs and mews so evenly kept time,
She purred in metre and she mewed in rhyme."

JOSEPH GREEN

"The way to keep a cat is to try to chase it away."

E. W. HOWE

"Far in the stillness a cat languishes loudly."

WILLIAM E. HENLEY, In Hospital

"The tail, in cats, is the principal organ
of emotional expression."

ALDOUS HUXLEY

"Cats and monkeys, monkeys and cats—
all human life is there."

HENRY JAMES, The Madonna of the Future

"A domestic animal that catches mice, commonly reckoned by naturalists the lowest order of the leonine species."

SAMUEL JOHNSON

"Helter skelter hang sorrow, care'll kill a cat, up-tails all, and a louse for the hangman."

BEN JONSON, *Every Man in His Humour*

"More ways of killing a cat than choking her with cream."

CHARLES KINGSLEY, *Westward Ho*

"Cats are intended to teach us that not everything in nature has a purpose."

GARRISON KEILLOR

"He will kill Mice and he will be kind to Babies when he is in the house, as long as they do not pull his tail too hard."

RUDYARD KIPLING, *Just-So Stories*

"The wildest of all the wild animals was the Cat. He walked by himself, and all places were alike to him."

RUDYARD KIPLING, *Just-So Stories*

"It is as easy to hold quicksilver between your finger and thumb as to keep a cat who means to escape."

ANDREW LANG

"If a fish is the movement of water embodied, given shape, then a cat is a diagram and a pattern of subtle air."

DORIS LESSING

"No matter how much cats fight, there always seem to be plenty of kittens."

ABRAHAM LINCOLN

"The cat is not a socially living animal . . . it is not my prisoner, but an independent being of almost equal status who happens to live in the same house that I do."

KONRAD LORENZ

"With their qualities of cleanliness, discretion, affection, patience, dignity, and courage, how many of us, I ask you, would be capable of being cats?"

FERNAND MERY

"When I play with my cat, who knows whether I do not make her more sport than she makes me? (. . . whether she is not amusing herself with me more than I with her?)"

MICHEL EYQUEM MONTAIGNE, *Essais*

"Cats sit in laps because it's warm there. They don't care if it's you or the radiator."

HENRY MORGAN

"Cats are intended to teach us that not
everything in nature has a purpose."

"The playful kitten, with its pretty little tigerish gambols, is infinitely more amusing than half the people one is obliged to live with in the world."

LADY SYDNEY MORGAN

"I call my kittens 'Shall' and 'Will' because no one can tell them apart."

CHRISTOPHER MORLEY

"We cannot, of course, without becoming cats, perfectly understand the cat-mind."

ST. GEORGE MIVART, FELINE ANATOMIST

"The trouble with a kitten is that eventually it becomes a cat."

OGDEN NASH

"It would have made a cat laugh."

JAME ROBINSON PLANCHÉ, VICTORIAN PLAYWRIGHT

"But thousands die, without or this or that, Die, and endow a college, or a cat."

ALEXANDER POPE, "MORAL ESSAYS"

"A kitten is chiefly remarkable for rushing about like mad at nothing whatever, and generally stopping before it gets there."

AGNES REPPLIER

"If 'The child is father of the man,' why is not
the kitten father of the cat?"
AGNES REPPLIER

"All cats love fish but fear to wet their feet."
WILLIAM SHAKESPEARE, *Macbeth*

"Cats are a mysterious kind of folk. There is more
passing in their minds than we are aware of."
SIR WALTER SCOTT

"I am as vigilant as a cat to steal cream."
WILLIAM SHAKESPEARE, *King Henry IV*, PART I

"They'll take suggestion as a cat laps milk."
WILLIAM SHAKESPEARE, *The Tempest*

"A kitten in the animal world is what
a rosebud is in the garden."
ROBERT SOUTHEY

"I could have persuaded myself that the word
felonious is derived from the feline temper."
ROBERT SOUTHEY

"The phrase 'domestic cat' is an oxymoron."

"There is a ridiculous idea that dogs are superior to cats because cats cannot be trained. A cat will not jump into a lake and bring back a stick. Would you?"

ROBERT STEARNS, *Cat Catalog*

"She watches him, as a cat would watch a mouse."

JONATHAN SWIFT

"I have studied many philosophers and many cats. The wisdom of cats is infinitely superior."

HIPPOLYTE TAINE

"Cats, like cars, tend to get stolen, scratched, and weather-worn if parked outside night after night."

DAVID TAYLOR, *The Cat: An Owner's Maintenance Manual*

"I will be deafer than the blue-eyed cat, And thrice as blind as any noon-tide owl"

ALFRED, LORD TENNYSON, *The Idylls of the King*

"A kitten is so flexible that she is almost double; the hind part is equivalent to another kitten with which the forepart plays. She does not discover that her tail belongs to her until you tread on it."

HENRY DAVID THOREAU

"If man could be crossed with the cat, it would improve man, but it would deteriorate the cat."

MARK TWAIN

"The cat that sits down on a hot stove-lid . . . will never sit down on a hot stove-lid again—and that is well; but also she will never sit down on a cold one."

MARK TWAIN

"A house without a cat, and a well-fed, well-petted, and properly revered cat, may be a proper house, perhaps, but how can it prove its title?"

MARK TWAIN

"Ignorant people think it's the noise which fighting cats make that is so aggravating, but it ain't so; it's the disgusting grammar they use."

MARK TWAIN

"Of all God's creatures there is only one that cannot be made the slave of the leash. That one is the cat."

MARK TWAIN

"If a dog jumps into your lap, it is because he is fond of you; but if a cat does the same thing, it is because your lap is warmer."

ALFRED NORTH WHITEHEAD

> "Like a graceful vase, a cat, even when motionless, seems to flow."
>
> GEORGE WILL

> "The phrase 'domestic cat' is an oxymoron."
>
> GEORGE WILL

> "The real objection to the great majority of cats is their insufferable air of superiority."
>
> P. G. WODEHOUSE

FOREIGN WORDS FOR "CAT"

The word for cat in ancient Greece was *ailourus*, which meant "the waving ones," referring to their tails.

The Latin word *cattus* (or *catus*) first appeared in the fourth century in a treatise by Palladius. (The earlier Roman word *Felis* referred to weasels and martens, as well as cats.)

African   *Kadis, Katsi*
Arabic   *Kitte, Otta, Quit, Quttah, Qatt, Biss*
Armenian   *Gatz*
Byzantine Greek   *Katos*
Catalan   *Gat*
Chinese   The words for "cat"—*mao, mio, mauk,* and *miu*—are all onomatopoetic, that is, they are derived from the perceived sounds that a cat makes.
Danish   *Kat*

Dutch Kat
Egyptian Kut
Filipino Pusa
Finnish Kissa, Poes
French Chat
German Katze
Greek Kata, Catta, and Ga'ta
Hawaiian Popoki, Owan
Hebrew Chatul
Hindi Billy
Icelandic Köttur
Indonesian Kutjing, Puss
Italian Gatto
Japanese Neko
Latin Cattus
Malay Kucing
Maltese Qattus
Norwegian Katt
Nubian Kadiz
Polish Kot
Portuguese Gato
Romanian Pisicá
Russian Koshka
Spanish Gato
Swahili Paka
Swedish Katt, Katta
Syrian Qatì
Thai Meo
Turkish Kedi
Vietnamese Meo
Ukrainian Kotuk
Welsh Kath
Yiddish Kats

PUSSYCAT POTPOURRI

The word "cat" used by jazz musicians, as in "he's a hep cat," does not have anything to do with felines. According to language expert J. L. Dillard, the word can be traced to a West African word "kat" which means "man" or "person" and "hepkat" means "person who can see clearly."

A temple, Go-To-Ku-Ji, dedicated to cats is located in Tokyo, Japan. It contains many images of cats (carvings, paintings, etc.) and is the burial site of some cats.

French kings Louis XI, Henry IV, Louis XIII and Louis XIV attended the Fires of St. John festivals on the first Sunday of Lent and St. John's Eve in June, during which a few dozen live cats were burned to death. Louis XIV abolished the practice after he reigned over the 1648 "festival," although the practice continued in the provinces until 1796, the Directory period of the French Revolution. These fiery festivities were supposed to ensure good crops and chase away droughts and bad storms.

Cats are well known for not taking to the leash as dogs do, but among the breeds that are more apt to handle a leash are the Siamese, Burmese, Russian Blue, colorpoint shorthairs, and Oriental shorthairs.

Cat (and dog) ownership helps convalescing people recover and tends to lower blood pressure. Heart attack victims who own pets greatly increase their chances of surviving longer than non-owners.

The only domestic animal not mentioned in the Bible is the cat.

In Greek mythology, Apollo, the sun god, created the lion, and his sister Artemis, the moon goddess, created the cat.

In Norse mythology, the cat is associated with the goddess of fertility and wealth, Freyja. Freyja is often depicted driving a chariot driven by two cats.

English poet Thomas Gray wrote the unusual "Ode on the Death of a Favorite Cat Drowned in a Tub of Gold Fishes."

English poet Christopher Smart wrote the poem "Jubilate Agno" about his pet cat Jeoffrey.

Cats occasionally appear on family coats of arms. Some of the families include the names Adams, Brockmann, Chaffaux, Chaurand, Chazot, Heigl, Katzeler, and Pachahamer. Lions, of course, appear in many coats of arms.

The "cat" in CAT scan stands for Co-Axial Tomography.

When a cat holds its tail straight up, it is a sign of welcome. When it sways the tail from side to side, it is agitated. When its tail is between its legs, it is frightened.

To a pilot, CAT means Clear-Air Turbulence, which is high altitude wind turbulence when no visible weather or meteorological indicator is apparent.

ABOUT THE AUTHOR

Ed Lucaire is the author of several fun fact books, including *Celebrity Setbacks*, *The Celebrity Almanac*, *Phobophobia*, *Joan Embery's Amazing Animal Facts* (co-author), *Famous Names for Your Pampered Pet*, and *Celebrity Trivia*. He is a graduate of Amherst College and is an avid collector of facts.

About his book with Joan Embery of the San Diego Zoo, *People* magazine wrote, "She and Lucaire have rounded up an alphabetical directory of animal trivia that is readable and handy if not full of zoological revelations . . . all fun. All manner of beasties, from aardvarks to zebras, amaze in Joan Embery's *Animal Facts*." *Library Journal* wrote, "Interesting bits of information . . . presented in a very clear, pleasant and straightforward manner . . . beautifully illustrated with realistic drawings of animals."

Lucaire's articles, reviews, and excerpts have appeared in *New York* magazine, *The New York Times*, *Spy* magazine, *Reader's Digest*, *The Wall Street Journal*, and *Games*.